Stories About Man and Nature

Book Two

THE ORPHANED DUCKLINGS

and Other Tales

CARL EWALD

Translations and Adaptations

William V. Zucker

Illustrations

Subhadeep Ghosh

© 2021 WILLIAM V. ZUCKER / Translator

Available in these formats:
978 1-7357216-2-0 (Paperback)
978 1-7357216-3-7 (eBook)

Library of Congress Control Number: 2020918143

Editing: Graham W. Schofield
Cover Design/Illustrations: Subhadeep Ghosh

Published by the translator
Forgeus Press / Tucson, Arizona 85716   U.S.A.
Phone: 520-327-0192

williamzucker@msn.com

www.classicnaturestoriesforkids.com

Other Translations by William V. Zucker

The Disobedient Owl / Book One
Carl Ewald

The Unfortunate Carp! / Book Three
Carl Ewald

The Invincible Sea / Book Four
(Coming 2021)
Carl Ewald

Five Children's Stories /A Learning Guide
(Coming 2021)
Carl Ewald & William V. Zucker

The Children's Crusade: A Synopsis /
Carl Ewald

Danish Fairy Tales & Rhymes /
Anna S. Seidelin

To Les and Lon

... stories I wish I had read to you.

Translator's Introduction...

A long with the need to entertain... parents, teachers, librarians and to all who value quality reading for children, this book offers ten stories that have a common theme: Man and Nature.

This is the second book in a series that feature fable-tales of stories for children, offering a penetrating glimpse of a faithful-to-nature world and its many creatures, plant and animals.

The highly acclaimed author of these stories, Carl Ewald (1856-1908), wrote them in Denmark over 100 years ago. His early training as a field biologist and forester gave him huge insights into nature and spurred an interest that lasted throughout his life.

These amazing stories are as valid today as they were in his time, and they offer so much to a new generation of children throughout the English-speaking world. They inform, they teach, and they stimulate the imagination

Charles Darwin, with his theory of evolution through natural selection, was a near contemporary of the author. He informed and enthused Ewald who quickly embraced these ideas in his writings for children and penned twenty collections of nature stories.

In the years that have passed since these stories first appeared, it is apparent that man has both worked positively—establishing National Parks and Monuments and the UNESCO World Heritage

Sites, for two examples—as well as negatively through seeming environmental ignorance that impacts and even desecrates the natural world and its creatures.

In his time, Carl Ewald saw that impact as an impending tension that would test our resolve to respect nature as one of man's most precious keepsakes. Whether it is our forests, our oceans, our feathered friends, our wild animals or fields of grain, they are all affected by the decisions and actions of man. Ewald entreated us to accept that responsibility with care and compassion. He also strived to give children—and their elders—some needed advice regarding how to interpret and understand the give and the take of our relationship with nature.

Most of Ewald's stories remain untranslated into English, but not all, and thus I am not the first to take on this task. However, my versions adapted from the original Danish are intended to be the most modern and relevant to children in the 21st Century.

This second book of stories is a sampling of not just the sweep of Ewald's interest in revealing a real-world nature, but also the high literary quality of his stories. There are many more stories, and I can't wait to bring them all to you.

My sincerest thanks to Erling and Lis Pilgaard for help with translation chores. For invaluable guidance and help with the text, I thank Graham Schofield, and to Subhadeep Ghosh, my sincerest gratitude for his outstanding illustrations and book cover design, but especially for his patience and appreciation of how text and visuals need to coalesce.

William V. Zucker
Tucson, Arizona - U.S.A.
2021

When you finish reading this book...
would you please write a review!

Authors (and translators)
love hearing from their readers.

To help other readers and children find these realistic descriptions of nature by Carl Ewald, let the translator know what you thought about the stories in this book.

Please leave an honest review on Amazon or Goodreads or your other preferred online store.

(If you are under 14, please ask a grown-up to help you).

Thank you!

P.S. Please mention
what your favorite story was.

www.amazon.com
www.classicnaturestoriesforkids.com

Choose your story...

The Fox's Last Stand

Chapter 1

It was fall. The leaves were getting yellow, falling, and crackling in the air. The rowan fruits were hanging down, round and red. The hawthorns and blackthorns were full of berries, the sun was high in the sky. The forest was lovely.

But the fox didn't think so.

The hop poles were set up with wisps of straw all around, and the fox knew all about that. It meant that the hunting season would soon be in swing, and there would be shooting and popping, screaming and yelling, thumps on trees, just a really horrible period. And you also risked your life. For sure, the fox had avoided his fate up until now, but who knew how long that could last? Fifteen of his kittens and his first mate had fallen in sacrifice—murdered—and maybe now it would be his turn.

It wasn't easy either to avoid the men with beaters who stood close to each other during the hunt. If you were even driven in the direction of the hunters, you might just as well throw in the towel right away. If the first shot went by you, then the second would probably hit you. And the very worst part of it was when you were shot and wounded but not killed. An old fox had walked around like that here for over a year. His left hind leg was badly shot up, but he managed to escape and came out of it with his life. For over a year he hobbled around, unable to procure himself anything to eat until he lay down in a field of rye and died. He laid there until he rotted.

That's almost worse than a quick death by a hail of shot.

The fox walked slowly through the woods, looking around from hop pole to hop pole. This was where the first fox drive with beaters would start, and then the hunters would have lunch, and commence to the next fox drive. The fox knew about all this because he had witnessed many hunting parties. And even if you're the big prize at end of the hunt, you learn a great deal about survival if you have your head in the right place, which was the case for the fox.

He thought it was smartest to remain in his den. When the hunters advanced with their beaters, they were without their dachshunds, so it was best to stay below ground until it was all over. Sure, he was hungry, but he'd get over it, and in any event, he had been hungry before, and one day's hunger was far preferable to certain death. And he had an uneasy feeling that this time he'd better remain where he was. He was no longer so young, nor so fast.

He didn't think that he could make those nimble jumps anymore, which saved him the last time.

No sooner said than done. Shortly after, the fox was sitting in his den waiting for whatever was yet to happen.

He could clearly hear the crack of the rifles, and the sound of the beaters in the woods. But it didn't tempt him at all. He laid with his head on his front paws far enough forward at the exit hole to make out the opening, but not be seen himself. And as he now lay there waiting, with his guts screaming at him, dying of hunger, two hares came by and sat down just outside his den.

"They must be utterly insane," thought the fox, but didn't budge from the spot, lying as still as a mouse.

And the two hares were also very quiet. They had romped around so much that both their long-eared heads were swimming. The bullets whizzed around their ears, and one of them had gotten so close to a man with a beater that it received a blow over its back from his stick. In vain, they tried to escape from the chain of hunters, but everywhere there was somebody. They were now sitting in the midst of the turmoil expecting only that their last hour had come. They waited on a hill overgrown with low shrub, which didn't even reach high enough to cover their long ears.

"God help and protect me," one of them said. "We're sitting right outside a fox's hole."

"What's the difference where we sit," said the other hare mournfully. "Do you think it's any better to be shot by a hunter than eaten by a fox? Besides the fox is shot; I saw him lying here before looking dead as a doornail."

"Goodness, there are other foxes besides me," said the fox to himself. "I wonder how old these hares are. If they're still young, I wouldn't mind snapping up one of them. It's a super idea to sit down here and feast on hare while they're shooting up above.

Anyway, the shots are coming more frequently and much more of them. It's probably much too risky to snatch a hare, but I certainly can move a bit closer to them."

He crawled soundlessly toward the exit hole where the hares were sitting. They didn't notice it, intent as they were on their fears, and also convinced that the fox was dead. As the shots came ever closer, they continued to sit and talk in their distress.

"Goodness, who has it better than the fox," said the other hare. "He has teeth that he can bite with and doesn't need to fear any other animals in the woods. And if the hunters chase him, he has his den deep in the ground to which he can retreat, and it has two or three exits."

"I have actually four," said the fox to himself, "but the forest ranger knows the location of all of them, so they aren't any more useful than one."

"How can you say that the fox has it so easy?" said the first hare. "Would you really want to be such a sneaky, contemptible fox that all the forest's animals fear, and whom they hate because of his cruel and cunning character?"

"There, I'll be dammed, here comes that story again," said the fox to himself. "Just like with the nightingale. They're all equally ridiculous with their make-believe. But just you wait until I get you between my teeth, my cabbage-eating friend. You'll feel my contempt all right."

"Okay," said the first hare. "Then I'd rather be a poor, persecuted hare living honestly by eating vegetables and not causing any grief to a mother's soul. It's a totally different, but decent way to live."

"Of course," said the fox. "The cabbage and all the other green vegetables you eat have no special permission to live, and you're a fine fellow when you munch on them just because they don't scream, but I'm a sneaky thief when I eat you. But now... now I'm going to get you."

The fox jumped out of his hole, and bit one of the hares in the neck. At the same moment, a shot was heard, and the second hare rolled over dead. Quickly, the fox was back in his den with his hare, shaking and stretching to see if one of the bullets had hit him. But amazingly, he was unscathed.

"It worked," said the fox, "and now I have enough food to last out the siege even if it takes a week."

He began eating the hare but lifted up his head and listened. There were voices outside, and he crawled with his prey as close to the entrance as he could in order to hear what was happening. He realized at once that the hunters had assembled just outside his den. They were standing around looking casually at the dead hare they had shot. Then one of them whistled, and some people came forward with lunch baskets and they sat down around the fox's den and began to eat. One of them stuck his boot down into the fox's den, kicking the gravel loose.

"You pig," said the fox. "You're kicking up sand on my hare."

"I'm pretty sure that there's a fox here," said one of the hunters. "Just as I was shooting the hare, I saw a fox leaping. Maybe he's in this hole."

"That's not unlikely," said the forest ranger. "An old fox does live here, the smartest one in the whole forest. I could never get a good shot at him, and he's stolen many a good chicken from me. He's done rearing his kids, and we got two of them this morning on the first beating drive. But I expect that it's not impossible that he'll be smart enough to keep inside his den the entire day."

"You sure know your business" said the fox, "and you sure know all about my family's situation. I wonder if you can smell that I'm eating a hare, you old ranger. How I've tricked you so many times! I must admit that your chickens are tastier."

"There are too many foxes in the woods here," said the forest ranger. "We've only gotten two today by using beaters, and we'll hardly catch any more this time. Those fellows are too clever—but this one now, I am going to get him. I've acquired two new dachshunds that should be well up to the job. Real early tomorrow morning, I'm going out with them and I have a feeling we'll come back with this fox fellow. Here are the four exits. We'll put one of the hounds down each of these two holes, while an assistant and I watch out for the other two. But we have to get early up in the morning to get the better of him."

"You can try that," said the fox to himself. "But I'm afraid that you'll have to remain awake starting now if you intend to derive any fun from your lovely plan. Forest ranger, I know one old fox at least who isn't going to sleep home tonight."

The hunters ate their lunch quietly, and the fox ate the hare. When the hunters finished, the fox was also done. When the hunters were gone, the fox came out of his den, laid down in the sunshine, and slept soundly. He knew that all danger had passed him by—this time.

Chapter 2

When the hunting party was over, and everything had settled down in the forest again, the fox awoke, stretched and yawned. Sitting on his tail, he considered his next move.

It was certain that the forest ranger would come back with his two well-trained hounds and his assistant just like he had planned. Admittedly, he was now having dinner at the manor house, and that might drag on. But he was a man to get up early anyway, healthy old specimen that he was, and the type who once something enters his head, acts on it. He wouldn't come in the wee hours of the night because he knew the fox was out. He knew the fox's lifestyle as well as he knew his own. He knew that the fox came back just before sunup, and shortly after that he would arrive with his entourage.

Now of course it was out of the question that the fox would remain home waiting for that wonderful visit. True enough, he had shamelessly bitten one of the ranger's hounds at some point so that it could never serve as a sniffing hound again, but just hobbled around at home in the farmyard like a pitiful invalid living on the dole and doing absolutely nothing for it. And, of course, the fox could try again, despite having gotten a few years older since then. But two hounds were more than one and they were supposedly well-trained. And then, the two marksmen. The assistant might well miss his mark because he was young and impulsive, but not the ranger himself. He had only missed his mark once before, going for the fox. And presumably his anger derived much more from that experience than from losing his chickens, because old man that he was, he was not stupid, and understood clearly that everyone had to live and look after his own interests.

But as already mentioned, there wasn't any reason to wait for the visit, nor did the fox intend to. He was also perfectly aware that it would not do to just return again to his den, and that was the most annoying aspect of it all. The den was a good one; he had lived in it for a long time and had feasted on many a good meal down there. First of all, the hounds would certainly totally mutilate it; secondly, the forest ranger would naturally return on another dawn. And then it was unlikely that he'd be forewarned, as he was this time.

So, he had to flee. A stretch away in the woods, he knew that there was a very nice den that belonged to his cousin who had dug it himself. He was shot and killed by hunters last year, and since then the den had been empty. Consequently, the fox sneaked away via some obscure paths that he knew so well, found the den again, and settled in. In practice, this meant that he had to pee and poop in front of each of the entry ways. Then the other foxes would know that the den was occupied by someone else. And of course, the badger also had to know this too, which was essential since he seldom cared to dig his own den, stealing it from foxes instead. And after a badger had lived in a den, even for only a day, no self-respecting fox would occupy it—the stench was something else. And that's not to mention that a badger was brave enough to defend himself before thinking about leaving.

When finally, everything was taken care of, you'd think that the fox would accept his new house and keep a very low profile, as much because he was totally stuffed with hare from yesterday; he didn't need to think more about food. But that wasn't the least bit his intention.

The very first thing he did was walk back to his old den and drag away as many discarded hawthorn branches as he was able to, and stuff them down into the two holes where he knew the dachshunds would dig. He figured that they'd be the two smaller holes. The forest ranger and the assistant would position themselves in front of the other holes. The hawthorn branches were easy to get, since a nearby forest fence had been cut down. He stuffed them in as tightly and completely as he was able, wholly certain that they'd have their hands full with them. On top of that, he decided next to tease the forest ranger a bit for his nasty planning. So, he laid down to sleep on a nice, warm mossy spot from which he knew he could be easily seen from the road, the same road that the forest ranger would take. He remained there throughout the night, sleeping with one eye shut and the other one glued to the road until dawn came.

The sun was hardly up before the fox saw the entourage make quite an entrance from the ranger's headquarters. The forest ranger was in the lead with his double-barreled shotgun half-cocked, both barrels filled with special shot for foxes, and knowing this, made the fox chuckle just thinking about it. The ranger was trailing the two hounds behind on a leash; or rather they were practically trailing him because they were so excited to get going that he could barely hold them back. Then came the assistant with his rifle. Near the end, the ranger's two other hounds, Diana and Apollo, were also along, for safety's sake, but also because it would be good for them to see how an old fox could be captured in its own den. At the very tail end, a little behind the others, Old Flux, the hound that had been bitten in its time by the fox, was hobbling along. He had presumably caught a whiff that this expedition dealt with the life of his mortal enemy and wanted to come along to see his demise.

"This time I think we'll get him," said the forest ranger. "There won't be any peace in the forest either before that old scoundrel is dead."

"He too," said the fox to himself. "These guys are all really something. He eats chicken, roast hare and venison every other day, and roast beef, veal, or lamb the rest of the time. And he calls me a thief and a bandit. When all is said and done, he's not a whit smarter than the pathetic nightingale I ate the other day. But all the better for me."

The hunting party disappeared into the woods, and the fox stood up from the thicket. He had made a long detour, so he was sure that none of the hounds picked up his scent. As the last sounds of the hunters were disappearing, he set about his work.

He jogged over the stubble field as fast as he could in the direction of the ranger's place. He didn't need to worry himself because he knew that all the hounds were in the woods, and there were no other farms in the vicinity. The farm hands were probably taking an extra snooze after they had helped the forest ranger get going, and they knew it could take a couple of hours or more before the ranger would return.

Quietly the fox entered the farmstead through a little alleyway that led to the henhouse. He knew that all the chickens were sitting on the perch asleep, as he also knew that they'd soon arouse and wake up everyone on the farm with their screaming. He had to work quickly. Just outside the henhouse was the now empty doghouse where Old Flux slept. Then there was a hatch that the chickens used for getting outside, but the hole was large enough for the fox to slip in. He had done it before.

And so, in he went, and in five minute's time, bit right through the throat of every hen there, never eating even one of them because he wasn't hungry; he did want to show the ranger just what the old fox was capable of doing.

"Now you'll see some nastiness," he said.

Chapter 3

So, the ranger and his entourage walked as quietly as a mouse. The hounds pushed forward on their leashes but didn't make a sound. They knew just as well as the others what was at stake. And Old Flux hobbled up to the top of the hill under which lay the fox den. There he sat and remained sitting with his tongue hanging out of his mouth. From that vantage point he could see all four entry ways and luxuriate at the sight of his mortal enemy receiving his comeuppance.

Soon every man was at his post. The forest ranger and the assistant cocked the triggers on their shotguns, and each stood by his hole. The two hounds were released and at the given signal charged down into the entryways.

Instantly they came back up with bloody snouts. Least of all had they expected to find hawthorn branches down there, and so they had rushed in ready to sink their teeth into the fox. The ranger scratched himself on the head. He couldn't figure this out. That the fox had abandoned the den was of course a possibility he had to consider. But he knew for sure that the fox had been there in recent days, but where the hawthorn twigs came from was a total mystery.

Meanwhile he urged the hounds down again into the holes, and they sniffed, yelped, dug, and finally bit right through the hawthorn twigs.

"Watch out," shouted the ranger to the assistant. "He's coming now...either to you or to me. I can hear him."

And something did appear at each hole—namely, a hound. The ranger saw at once what had happened, and annoyingly locked the trigger on his shotgun. But the assistant fired brazenly away at anything coming out of the hole he was assigned to watch. And this time he hit it, but he had just shot stone-dead one of the newest and best hounds in the business. The ranger fumed and raged, and the assistant was flummoxed, all of which, however, did nothing to bring back the life of the hound.

So, the hunting party started homeward, crestfallen, tired, discouraged and angry. Old Flux limped behind with his tongue hanging out of his mouth. "Just wait, you old fox," said the enraged ranger clenching his fist toward the forest. "I'll get my hands on you someday."

And so, he arrived home and found his daughter and the servant girl weeping, and the hired hand almost ready to keep them company. They were standing around the twenty-seven fat hens that they had laid in a row in the farmyard. All of them were stone-dead, with their throats slit. "Now I know where that old fox was last night," said the ranger, "and if I don't have his skin hanging on the wall over there before winter is over, then I'm not an honest forest ranger."

Chapter 4

Winter came, and it was a punishing one, fiercer than it had been for many, many years.

There wasn't a watering hole anywhere that wasn't frozen right to the bottom. The swiftest flowing brook in the woods was iced and bound over. And ice covered the ocean as far as the eye could see. Snow came, but not before the frost had already been there, biting to death what living life it could. The snow tumbled down hour after hour, day after day. And then the storm arrived bringing huge drifts that covered both paths and roads. Trees groaned from top to bottom, and those that had hollow places in them, those trees toppled to the ground.

The forest ranger's dwelling, which lay in a valley, was almost totally buried in snow. They had to dig their way through the gate. The sleigh with bells was brought out along with red and white nets and feather ornaments on the horses' heads. It was lovely and joyous for those who could amuse themselves, and also had the time to look forward to the frivolities. But for those who had to work, it was a tough time, and there were many who suffered miserably that winter.

And that was the case for the old fox, even more so.

He was of course also snowed under in the den. And he obviously couldn't just dig himself out as the ranger and peasants did. He had to really watch out for himself ever since the henhouse raid episode and the hound that was shot, because now the ranger was livid. Ever since the failed hunt, he had thought of nothing but the fox. At all hours he roamed through the woods, and while true enough, he had not yet found the den, he had gotten pretty damn close to it. And the fox reflected sometimes that he certainly could not escape in the long run.

And if he had simply moved the snow away from the entrance to the den, the ranger could have easily found it. Almost surely, he had not been in the woods since the last big snowfall, but no one could tell when he would come, and he was as tough as nails and as mad as a stinging bee.

So, the fox dug a long tunnel under the snow, around the hill, and a little tiny, innocent hole as far away as possible from the real entryway, and in a place that seemed unpretentious. There was only the inconvenience that the ceiling of snow would occasionally fall down blocking off the tunnel, so it had to be cleaned out again, which he did. But he sneezed point-blank from the snow and tripped with his paws when the water splashes came up under him in places where the frost couldn't get in. He deeply wished that the weather would soon turn reasonable again.

But if it was hard to hide the entryway to the den, and then the snow gave him a great deal more to worry about in another way.

For no matter where the old fox stepped, there were his tracks in the snow. They remained there in the clear frosty weather, hardened up, and looked as if they were carved in stone. And every farm boy could recognize them, let alone the forest ranger. If one day he was walking through the woods with his fur boots on, along with his horrible long shotgun that always hung over his shoulder, he'd catch a glimpse of something he longed for in years. He would see the hare's tracks, followed by the fox's. He'd think: 'Now that blasted fox has eaten one of my hares again.' But he'd be quite wrong because the fox had followed the hare's tracks but couldn't find the hare. God only knows where it went. It probably sat in a ditch somewhere frozen to death. Or maybe it had run out onto the ice in hopes of reaching a more hospitable area and had been shot to death by one of the beachcombers that picked off wild ducks there, night and day.

The ranger would also see how the snow was scraped to the side here and there at the base of the big beech trees. The fox's tracks led right to them, so there could be no doubt that he had done it. The ranger would think: "The old scoundrel is getting really desperate since he is now lying in wait for the mouse to come out of his hole. I like that mouse even if he's also a bandit. Let the fox eat as many mice as he needs to keep going until I can catch up with him one day and thank him—for the last time—with a hail of fire from my rifle."

But the ranger would have drawn a totally wrong conclusion again, because the fox hadn't captured a single mouse. He had for sure piled the snow out to the side in order to lie down and wait. He had also concealed himself on the other side of the tree trunk using every ounce of fox cunning he had. But it hadn't helped him in the slightest. The mouse never even considered that the fox was up above ready to eat him, if he came out. What in the world would he want to come out of his cozy hole for? He had his delicious food down there, and ate, slept and let the winter rage away in the forest.

The situation was simply that the fox was on the verge of dying of hunger. For the past week, the fox had nourished himself with only some horrible, bitter blackthorn berries which on top of it had scratched his snout badly as he tried to get hold of them. This couldn't go on for the long haul; he was so emaciated; it was shocking to see. He longed for a chicken, a hare, a mouse...even a not-too-thin little nightingale. But there was nothing. And the deep, white snow was not going away. The sun was shining a bit, but only to tease folks a little. In the night, the cold stars twinkled, and it was nasty outside.

Every night the fox went out to the edge of the woods from where on the hillside he could look down into the ranger's quarters. He spent many an agonizing hour there.

He thought about the twenty-seven hens whose throats he had slashed that day in order to tease the ranger. He wasn't hungry then, hadn't eaten a morsel, didn't drag a hen with him on the way home; he simply murdered them out of anger and revenge. What wouldn't he give if he hadn't done that, so that he could now sneak back and grab himself a delicious hen? That was to put your life at risk, of course, but that's better than slinking around in the woods with cold feet, waiting to die of hunger. He could have gotten himself a hen today, and another one tomorrow. Or perhaps it would have been smarter to be satisfied with one every other day because the day after a steal, folks are very much on edge. He'd take care of Flux. He could mutilate his other hind leg if he wanted to. Besides, Flux was probably asleep, and he could hardly see or hear anyway.

The fox licked his chops, salivating with hunger. It was only dreams and hunger hallucinations. There were no hens at the ranger's place, since he had bitten all twenty-seven of them to death himself for no reason at all. And the ranger had sworn that he wouldn't have a feathered creature in his yard until that old fox was shot. Otherwise, he was just feeding it.

So, in his desperation, the fox forgot his cunning. He bayed loudly and for a long time, so it could be heard far out in the countryside, and he ran home angry.

The ranger awoke in his bed, heard the baying, and laughed. "Ho, ho! you old sneaky fox," he said to himself. "Now you're hurting. But just wait. I'll make you hungrier yet."

*   *   *

One night, the fox went out to his usual spot at the edge of the woods, and to his great surprise he saw a large rooster lying on the snow. He was just about to jump on it when he quickly reconsidered and sat a little bit away from it to watch.

The rooster was dead; that was clear. He was also large and fat, and enormously appetizing. So far, there wasn't anything out of the ordinary. The only question was: How did it get there? There were no hens at the ranger's place which the fox knew better than anyone else. And on this side of the forest, there weren't any other farms it could have come from. How in the world had it managed to come all the way up here, only to lie down and die in the woods? It smelled of some kind of foul play—from the ranger, of course.

The fox withdrew a little further, still looking at the rooster. He wasn't born yesterday. He knew very well, for example, that there was something called a fox trap that was a very nasty experience.

On the other hand, he was so hungry that his head was spinning. He had to summon all his wits to prevent himself from rushing at the rooster without consideration.

As he was sitting there in his distress, he spotted a little chaffinch who was sitting all huddled up asleep in the crotch of a bent limb just over his head. The fox sputtered, the chaffinch awoke, and seeing the fox, it got such a fright that he nearly fell into his mouth.

"Good morning, chaffinch," said the fox.

"Shame on you for giving me such a fright," said the chaffinch. "I almost fell down on top of your head, and you would have eaten me."

"I don't really think so," said the old fox. "Not really. As I think about it, I'm quite sure that I wouldn't have eaten you."

"That's the kind of talk you tell all the finches," said the chaffinch. "But I know you well enough. There's not a more underhanded thief in the woods than you."

"Thank you," said the fox. "I know the tune. They all sing it the same way everywhere, in the forest and wherever. I don't care to defend myself against those charges. Indeed, I'll go so far as to admit that under different circumstances, I would have eaten you with great relish. But not tonight. Certainly not tonight."

"Why not?" asked the chaffinch. "Aren't you hungry?"

"Hungry?" said the fox. "Am I hungry? I'm dying of hunger. But I'm not going to eat a chaffinch if I can have a rooster. And there's a rooster lying in the snow over there. But I can't get it without your help."

"That's strange," said the chaffinch. "I can't figure that out. But, why should I help you? You've been very mean to us little birds. You're not eating me today because you didn't manage to get hold of me, but you've said yourself that you'd willingly eat me on another day. I'm not going to help you."

"Yeah, that's what I get for being so honest," said the fox. "By the way, I'm not asking a great amount of help from you. I'd just like you to tell me if you know how the rooster got here."

The chaffinch reflected momentarily on this. He hadn't any idea how the rooster had gotten there, but just like the fox, he, too, could put two and two together. He had also been entrapped in a snare once, lured by some rowan berries, and had escaped only by a miracle, so he understood exactly what the fox was so worried about. But he also wished the fox all the bad luck possible.

"How about it?" asked the fox.

"You mean the rooster?" said the chaffinch. "Of course, I know how it got there. I've been sitting here asleep all night. He just came flying in. Probably he was sick because he was complaining a lot when he landed on the snow. So, he was dying while I was asleep."

"Presumably," said the fox. "Was it also while you were asleep that those footprints appeared in the snow, possibly? They resemble the ranger's a great deal."

"I don't know anything about that," said the chaffinch. "No one that I know has been here except the rooster. But could someone have come here before the rooster? That's not impossible."

"They could have," said the fox. "Of course, they could have."

He sat there for a while thinking about it. He felt either he had to go and get the rooster or walk away from it. He wasn't going to stand this for much longer.

"Of course, the ranger could have set that rooster out for you," said the chaffinch.

"The ranger...put a rooster out for me?" said the fox. He had to laugh out loud at the thought.

"Sure, why not?" said the chaffinch. "The ranger is a good man. I was sitting in his walnut tree yesterday and watched while he and his hired hand shoveled the snow to the side, away from the cabbage. 'These are for my hares,' he said. 'Let them have them to eat or they'll all die on me in this horrible winter.' If he can be so considerate of the hares, he can also have a little warm spot for a fox."

The fox nodded his head. His brain was so befuddled by hunger that he couldn't even think straight.

Actually, why couldn't it be like the chaffinch said? The ranger hunted hares just like he hunted fox. While he ate the hare's flesh for food, he used the fox's fur for a foot warmer. He also enjoyed going hunting, and if the animals died due to the winter cold, then there wouldn't be anything left to hunt. True enough, he was especially furious at the fox, but for that reason he'd probably like to keep him alive until he could extract his revenge. Exactly, that was exactly how it was, of course. He was just going to provide the fox with some sustenance so that he would have the pleasure of shooting him later on.

The fox laughed loudly at the thought of fooling the ranger. And his ears buzzed with excitement as he lost all control of himself. In a leap, he was on top of the rooster, tearing at it so the blood was running from its mouth, and at the same time he let out an awful scream.

His left hind leg was caught in a fox-snare. If it had even been his tail, he could have dispensed with it, but not his hind leg. Besides, he was caught way up on the thigh, and so there was nothing to do about it. He was trapped, fooled in the shabbiest way possible.

The old fox ate the rooster. He had to do that right away. Then he looked up at the chaffinch who was sitting and shaking with glee.

"You little rascal," said the fox.

"You big rascal," said the chaffinch. "By the way, I'm not a rascal. I had no idea the rooster was a trap, but if I had known about it, I never in an eternity would have said anything to you. You deserve to have a bad experience for once and for all that you've got on your conscience, you sneaky fox."

The fox was hurting in the trap and didn't answer the chaffinch. It was ridiculous to respond. Chaffinches eat flies, foxes eat chaffinches, and forest rangers hunt foxes. Why was the fox a worse thief than the others? But nothing mattered any more now; it was all over. He had tried in a hundred different ways to break free, but it was impossible. The trap held him tightly. He also realized when he moved his leg that there was another snare that he could easily set off that would immobilize his other hind leg. So, he had to remain standing quietly the whole long night so as not to lie down. The stars shone down on him, the frosty air bit at him, and the chaffinch mocked him. He did think though about how stuffed he was again finally, and how scrumptious the rooster tasted.

As soon as it was light, the ranger came back. Even from a far distance, he saw that the fox was snared. He waved his hat in the air, cried hurrah, and urged on the hounds, the assistant, and the hired hand. Soon they were all standing around the captured fox, looking at him with rage in their eyes. "Well," said the ranger. "This old ranger has finally got the better of the old fox. "So, he gave the fox his *coup de grace* with his hunting knife—or so he thought.

But the fox was not actually completely dead. And when the ranger picked him up by his hind legs in order to carry him home, he suddenly let out a horrible shriek, and threw the fox down onto the snow

The fox had bit him in the calf. But that was the last thing the fox did. He was finally dead, was flayed, and ended up as a foot-warmer, or got hung on the ranger's cabin wall.

The Forest and the Heath

Chapter 1

Many years ago, there was a beautiful forest with thousands of upright tree trunks with numerous birdsongs and stirrings in their shady crowns, which made beautiful music as the breeze rippled through them.

Surrounding the forest was a field for planting, and a grassy meadow next to where the farmer had built his house. In the summertime, the field and the meadow stayed green and bright as the farmer was hard working and grateful for the crops that he brought home. But the revered forest towered over all of them.

In the wintertime, the field seemed neglected and pitiful under the snow, and the meadow was just a lonesome, iced-over lake. Inside the house, the farmer huddled over the stove in the corner. But even with its bare branches, the forest stood ever erect and peaceful with its bare branches, letting it storm and snow just as the weather pleased.

When spring came, both field and meadow turned green again, and the farmer came out to start plowing and sowing. By this time, the forest had sprung out in an indescribably beautiful display, and there were scents from gaily-colored flowers at its feet, and sun on its green carpet. Birdsongs were heard once more coming from the smallest bush, and it was a time for festivities far and wide.

One summer's day, while the forest was swaying with its branches, it noticed an odd-looking brown thing spreading itself on the hill to the west, something it had never seen before.

"What kind of a creature are you?" asked the forest.

"I am the heath," said the brown thing.

"I don't know you," replied the forest, "and I don't like you; you're so ugly and black, resembling neither field nor meadow, or anything I know. Can you bud out? Do you produce flowers? Can you make music?"

"Indeed, I can!" said the heath. "In the middle of August when your leaves darken and appear spent, my flowers spring out. Then I look red from top to bottom and more beautiful than anything you have seen."

"Braggart!" said the forest, and they stopped talking to each other.

By the following year, the heath had sprawled a long distance down the hill toward the forest. The forest took notice but said nothing. It considered it undignified to chat with such an ugly thing, but deep inside, it was really worried. Still, it turned even greener and appeared lovelier, as though there was not a thing to be concerned about. But for every year that passed, the heath encroached more closely, and now all the hillsides were covered, and it was lying right outside the forest's fence.

"Get away!" said the forest. "You're annoying me and watch out that you don't touch my fence!"

"I'm going over, around, and under your fence!" replied the heath. "I'll penetrate into you, consume you, and destroy you."

The forest laughed at this, making all its leaves quiver.

"So, that is what you're about?" it said. "If only you could manage it, but I'm afraid you're just outclassed. I suppose you think I'm just a trifling field or meadow you can spread over in a jiffy. But I'm the grandest and the noblest being in the whole countryside, I'll have you know. Now I'll sing you my song, and then maybe you'll have second thoughts."

So, the forest began to sing. All the birds sang, and the flowers lifted their petals and sang along. The smallest leaf hummed along with the others, the fox stopped in the middle of eating a fat hen, and kept time with its bushy tail; the wind raced through the branches providing an organ accompaniment to the forest's song:

I never saw a greater party,
Than the forest invited us to.
Then come the woodruff violet's aromas,
And the wild roses give some too.

Then flies the little birdie in the thicket
But never by itself.
The farmer decorates his beloved's bonnet,
With waving stems from the beech.

So happy are the hare, the fox and the deer,
The little worm under the swarm of petals;
The grown-ups dance, and the little ones dance,
And then the sun in the sky dances too.

"What do you think of that?" asked the forest.

The heath said nothing, but the next year it had moved over, around, and under the fence.

"Are you out of your mind?" screamed the forest. "I forbade you to come this far!"

"You are not my master," replied the heath. "I'll do what I want; I warned you."

So, the forest summoned the red fox and shook its branches so that a large number of its seeds fell down on top of the fox and remained stuck to its fur.

"Run out to the heath, little fox, and put the seeds there!" said the forest.

"I'm on my way," said the fox that sauntered off.

And the hare did the same, similarly the deer, the marten, and the mouse. And the crow, for the sake of old time's friendship, lent a hand too. The wind set about with a vengeance, shaking branches so that the acorns and beechnuts scattered far out into the heath.

"Now look," said the forest, "and let's see what will happen."

"Yes, let's!" said the heath.

Chapter 2

Time passed and the forest greened up and withered a little, but the heath kept spreading more and more. They didn't talk to each other now, but one beautiful spring day, tiny, newly sprouted beeches peeked up from the ground in the heather patch.

"What do you say now?" inquired the forest triumphantly. "My young trees will continue to grow year after year, becoming strong and tall. Then they'll close over you with their crowns; no sun will shine, no rain will fall upon you, and you'll die for your arrogance."

But the heath shook its black twigs severely. "You don't know me," it said. "I'm stronger than you think. Your trees will never green up in my patch. I've packed the ground under me; it is as strong as iron, and your roots will be unable to penetrate it. Just wait until next year. Those little fellows you're now so pleased with will die."

"You're lying," said the forest, but it was fearful.

The next year passed just as the heath had predicted. Every single small beech and all the oak saplings died; this was a terrifying experience to the forest. The heath kept spreading more and more, and everywhere the heather took the place of the violets and the anemones, too. There were no young trees growing, bushes withered, and the old trees started to die off at the tops; it was a total disaster.

"It's not very pleasant in the forest anymore," said the nightingale. "I think I'll find somewhere else to build and sing."

"There's hardly a decent tree to live in," said the crow.

"The ground has gotten so hard, you can't dig yourself a decent burrow," said the fox.

The forest didn't know what in the world to do. The beech stretched its branches up to the sky in prayer, asking for help, and the oak wrung its branches in quiet despair.

"Sing your song once more," said the heath. "I've forgotten it," said the forest mournfully. "And my flowers are withering; my birds flew away." "Then I shall sing," said the heath, and so, it did.

Listen to the story of the spreading heath,
When the sun arises in the east.
The heather blazes like fire and blood,
While the forest awaits the fall.

The cotton grass rambles all the long day,
In the bog, it's linen so white,
And the grass snake and viper with quiet wrigglings,
Softly glide under the heathers' tops.

Loudly wails the golden plover and the skylark trills,
The peewit rocks on little tufts.
The bent-over farmer walks so quietly,
Out from his house on the heath.

Chapter 3

As the years passed, the farmer left, his house fell into ruin, and the forest looked continuously worse. The heath kept spreading further until it reached the other end of the forest. The large trees died and fell as soon as the storm could get a firm hold on them. They laid there and rotted, and the heather grew over them. Only a dozen of the oldest and strongest trees was now standing, but they were all hollowed out, and had very sparse crowns.

"My time is over; I am dying," said the forest.

"Well, I told you that was coming," replied the heath.

Finally, the people nearby were terribly frightened about the way the heath was rushing quickly ahead, destroying the forest.

"Where will I get any wood for my workshop?" cried the cabinetmaker.

"Where will I get any sticks of wood to put under the frying pan?" screamed his wife.

"Where will I get any firewood for the winter?" sighed the old man.

"Where will I stroll with my girlfriend in the springtime?" said the young man.

After they had observed the old trees for a little while, about which they could do nothing, they picked up their shovels and picks and ran up the hills to where the heath began.

"You can spare yourselves the trouble," said the heath. I'm not fit to dig into."

"Oh no," sighed the forest. But it had become so weak now that no one else could hear what it was saying.

But the people didn't care about this. They chopped and chopped until they came through the hard layer. Then they put fresh earth into the holes, added fertilizer, and planted small trees. They tended them, believed in them, and defended them against the heath and the west wind as best they could.

Year after year, the small trees grew and they stood like light, green soldiers on parade in the middle of the black heather. Then, as time progressed, a little bird came around and built its nest in one of them.

"Hurrah! We have a forest again," exclaimed the people.

"No one can stand against humans," said the heath. "There's nothing we can do about it. Let's go elsewhere."

From the old forest, one tree was still standing with but a single green branch in its crown. In it, a little bird was talking about the new forest springing up over on the hill.

"Thank goodness," said the old forest tree. "What you can't achieve yourself, you must leave to your offspring. If only they're ready for it; they appear so thin."

"You were once thin yourself," said the bird.

The old forest did not reply to that, because, just then, its time on earth was finally over. It was time for the young ones to grow and take their place.

The Orphaned Ducklings

Chapter 1

It was winter. The leaves were gone from the trees, and the flowers from the fence hedges. Some birds had also left, the most distinguished ones in particular had traveled south, but some species remained behind. There was the common gray sparrow and the nimble little titmouse. The crow and the rook appeared doubly black and hungry against the white snow, and a couple of other types of birds decided to manage as best they could, rather than embarking on the long journey.

Down at the shore, it was even livelier than in the summer. Wherever there was a hole in the ice that formed where waters were shallow, sea gulls were romping around in large, noisy flocks everywhere, and wild ducks bobbed along in open waters before diving down to feed. When they had their fill, or heard the crack of the fishermen's rifle, they would take to the air in a flurry of wings.

"What a crowd!" said the gray sparrow.

"They come from up north," said the seagull. "From Norway and the Faeroe Islands. It's a hundred times colder up there than here, but as soon as there is just the slightest change in the air, they'll fly back up again. Do you know those two walking on the ice toward us?"

"Why would I know them?" replied the puzzled gray sparrow. "I was only born this summer, and right now, I wish I was back in the nest again." "It's the eider duck," said the seagull. "Look, there's another one coming."

One of them was a very elegant bird. Its nape was green, with a white neck, a rose-tinged breast, and lovely yellow-orange feet.

"That's the drake," said the seagull. "The other two are females, not as handsome of course, though they look all right."

The three eider ducks were now so close to the gray sparrow and the seagull that they could hear what they were talking about.

"Lovelies," said the drake. "I don't understand what you're doing here, way into the ice. Come along with me to the open waters and enjoy our company."

"I'm staying with my niece," said the aunt eider duck.

"And why won't the young Miss come with us?" inquired the dashing drake. "In the summer on our dear Faeroe Islands, you were the happiest of the happy."

The drake tried again for a minute to persuade her but without success and he then flew back over the ice.

"Isn't this place a *fjeld*, auntie?" said Miss eider duck, referring to the rocky, barren plateaus back home.

"If you don't mind my butting in, it's still cold enough right now," said the gray sparrow. "And we don't have any fjelds in this country."

"You can brood your eggs in the sand," said the seagull.

"Thank you for your information," said aunt eider duck, "but my niece is just getting a little anxious. She's three years old now and ready to mate."

"Heavens!" said the gray sparrow. "I was just born this summer, but I'm ready to find a mate right now if only it was a bit warmer."

"It's easier for some than others," said the aunt.

"Let's fly home to the Faeroe Islands and find mates," said the young Miss.

"In a month, my dear," said the aunt. "But I'll keep out of all that, thank you. I've been paired seven different times, and that's quite enough of that experience for me. But I would be happy to sit with you for a while and chat about it; it's often terribly interesting."

"In a month's time, the trees will still not be greened up," said the gray sparrow. "We're only just in January."

"We don't have any trees on the Faeroe Islands, my little friend," said the aunt. "And we don't need them either."

"Does Miss have an admirer?" asked the seagull.

"Not yet," said the aunt addressing the seagull, "but he'll come soon. We females can always get admirers. In the three years that my niece has lived, she has danced on the ocean and enjoyed herself. She has to get over that first."

"I only hope that she meets the right one," said the seagull.

"Males are all alike," said the aunt. "They woo us, mate with us, help possibly a bit with making the nest, and then take off, leaving all the rest to us."

"I don't agree with you," said the seagull. "My mate is dependably helpful."

"I've regularly gotten many flies from my father when I was still in the nest," said the gray sparrow.

"Then you've been luckier than the rest of us," said the aunt. "None of my seven mates have even so much as seen their own kids."

"Weird!" said the gray sparrow.

"Can't we go home to the Faeroe Islands soon?" asked Miss eider-duck.

"Goodness, how intense these youngsters are," said the aunt flapping her wings.

They then flew out into the water, but returned the next day, and this scene was repeated daily well into February. Young Miss eider duck really longed to fly home, and the aunt never grew tired of chatting with her about it.

"It is intolerable, it is insufferable!" the young Miss said. "It is so warm here, I can hardly stand it."

"I guess?" said the puzzled gray sparrow that was shivering and longing for spring.

One day a handsome young eider drake came by, stationing himself on the ice next to the two females.

"If he proposes, take him," whispered the aunt, looking straight at the young drake. "He has the greenest nape and head that I have seen in many years."

"If only he'll propose," whispered the young Miss.

And he did propose to her.

After sitting a while chatting about trivial things in order to appear polite—and acting politely doesn't require nearly so much effort with eider ducks as with people—he asked the young Miss if she would be his mate. He began to speak of the fjelds with birds on them, of small eggs and such, but she quickly interrupted him.

"Yes," she squealed, "I'd love to be your mate," and, just like that they were transformed into a new loving couple.

Needing to make a great impression, he swore that he would be a faithful mate all through their life together, he would build nests for her, sit on her eggs, and feed the young ones from morning to night. She nodded her head, unable to say anything because she was so deliriously happy.

"It's a lie, every blessed word he utters, but oh, how lovely it sounds," said the aunt.

"How terrible," said the gray sparrow and the seagull, uttering: "The sweet young thing."

"Nonsense!" said the aunt. "We've all been down that path. My seven mates all proposed that way, and not a one of them kept his promise. But they were all so sweet, only not as green as that one there. He's really cute. I'm about to fall in love with him myself."

"When are we leaving?" inquired the now happily mated eider duck.

"Tomorrow morning early, my love, if we have a good head wind," answered her new mate.

"I'm coming along," said the aunt. "First of all, it's quite convenient for me, and second, it's so lovely to see young love."

Chapter 2

They left the next morning. It was still dark as their flight began. Thousands of eider ducks were flying in flocks, and still other thousands joined them from all sides. The seagull and the gray sparrow woke up hearing chirping and singing in the air.

"They're going north in such cold weather," said the gray sparrow shivering. "It's freezing now worse than ever."

"Spring is in the air when you're in love," said the seagull.

Night and day the flight continued on its northerly course.

There were an unimaginable number of eider ducks in flight. Eventually as they approached closer to their destination, their longings for home grew so strong that they flew like there was a fire under their wings. The aunt did not veer from the two lovers and was just as strong in flight as they were, and equally enraptured as though she was about to enjoy her eighth mate.

Finally, they reached the Faeroe Islands, their summer home. They screamed and quacked for joy when they saw the fjelds rise up from the ocean, and their wings flapped even faster despite how tired they were from the long journey. They dispersed themselves over the rocks just like when on prowl for prey, and soon there wasn't a spot where a happy bird wasn't flapping its wings and shouting for joy.

"Now let me show you a good nesting site," said the aunt to the two youngsters who were sitting and looking lovingly at each other. "Follow me around to the other side of the fjeld." They flew with her and arrived at a place where the man who owned the fjeld had set up some small, scattered, hand-made wooden birdhouses just for the ducks. There was one still available, which the young drake occupied immediately.

"Here's where you can sit comfortably, and brood our eggs, my love," he said.

"Yes, and you too," she said. "Remember now that you promised me to share half of the work."

"Sure, I remember!" he replied, and embraced her.

"Oh, how lovely it is," said the aunt.

"Incidentally, I won't live in this horrible box," she said. "I have looked so forward to the two of us dragging up the seaweed, heather, and straw as you told me you've done with your other mates. And that's the way I want it too."

"Take it easy, my sweet," he said. "Of course, we'll line the box a little, but let's be happy that we have something to start off with. Remember now we have a long life ahead of us, full of hard work and much joy; let's not take on more than we can handle."

"Goodness, how he lies," said the aunt again, turning her eyes upward, "but it's so beautiful to hear."

"What did you say?" asked the newly promised mother-to-be.

"I said your mate has the most handsome green nape and head on all the Faeroes," said the aunt. "I'd like to bite it myself, but I'll leave you to your happiness."

She then flew off, quacking, as she flew down across the fjeld, splashing into the water with the others.

The two lovers started lining the box with whatever they could find. Afterwards, they cuddled warmly and joyfully, just like the many thousands of other eider ducks that were also joined together that same day.

"Heavens, how lovely it is to see all the youngsters," said the aunt, who toddled around visiting the couples with a bunch of old-timer females.

The young lovers were also doing well and were very happy. But after laying her first egg in the nest, they had a disagreement. He wanted her to accompany him down the fjeld while the egg was lying there. She had nothing against that idea, although she did think he could show a little more delight with the lovely green-grey egg she had laid.

"I'm reserving my feelings," he said. "Can you get used to it, please; I'm a regular guy, okay?"

On the other hand, she said it was out of the question to leave the egg exposed. They had to cover it with something. She plucked out some fine down feathers from underneath her wings and laid them over the egg. But when she asked him to donate his down feathers, he defiantly shook his head.

"I'm saving my feathers," he said. "You need to lay four more eggs, and when you're all done, I'll begin. I'll pluck myself bald if necessary in order to provide for our kids."

"Heavens, have mercy... how he goes on!" said the aunt who was standing a little distance away listening. "I know this story well from my own mates. They don't mean a word of it, but it sure warms an old heart to hear them say it."

The expectant mother followed her mate onto the beach where there was an awful lot of lively activity and festivity. There were all the males and their mates along with the older males and females that didn't have nests any longer. They dipped and dived, chatted, and told amusing stories to each other. The young one kept mostly to herself or spoke with the other females who were also unusually quiet. After a while, she knew for sure that she was going to lay another egg.

"Little guy," she said, "Come, let's go home. Another egg is coming."

"What a shame," her mate said as he was right in the middle of a quadrille with a couple of young flirts he knew from previous summers. These young flirts were not thinking about coupling up yet.

But he followed her up to the nest and she laid her egg. She plucked out more of her down feathers, while he spoke in a lovely and heartfelt way to her, and then they went out again for some fun because now he could never stay home at the nest.

Hardly had they gone halfway before she felt that something was wrong again and mentioned it to him.

"You'd better stay up at the nest" he said peevishly. "This running around isn't fun for me and it's hurtful to the kids' health."

"Will you stay with me?" she asked.

"I'll look in on you as often as I can," he said.

"And that's the way you keep your promise to me," she said, crying pitifully.

"My dearest little mate!" he said. "I can't help you in the slightest with those eggs. You alone have to lay those eggs; you must. The work that I have to do for you and our loving babies only begins after all the eggs are laid, and you start brooding them. And then, too, when the sweet, tiny darlings break out and need to be fed and shown how to carry on in the world. But until that time, I need to save all my energies, you understand. Then I'll sit on the eggs while you fly around having a grand time, playing down there with the others."

"Have you ever heard the likes of that!" said the aunt. "He talks so beautifully. You've certainly got yourself a lovely man."

The young mother-to-be turned back home alone to the nest and laid the third egg.

"I'll watch out for him, believe me," the aunt whispered to her expectant niece before flying down to the beach with the young father-to-be.

And then came the fourth egg and the fifth.

The expectant mother had plucked off all of her down feathers that could be spared, and they lay like a cozy, mousy-type mound surrounding the eggs. She sat on top of all of them and brooded and brooded. In the beginning, she went occasionally to the edge of the rocks and peeked down onto the beach where her mate was romping with the other drakes and with the flirts that didn't have any eggs to brood. But she did it less and less. She lost her appetite, got thin, but continued to brood her eggs. The aunt came by every day for a chat with her.

One day her mate came back to their nest. He looked very handsome with his green nape and head and sparkling eyes.

"Well, how's it going?" he asked.

"I despise you," she said. "Get out! I never want to lay eyes on you again. You have deceived me with your loveliest of promises but you haven't kept one of them. I've had to pluck all the needed down from my very own breast. Day in and day out, I sit here alone while you amuse yourself with that loose crowd down at the beach. You haven't brought me a morsel of food to eat."

"Well... now," he said, scraping his elegant, orange-yellow feet in the ground. "I'll be happy to bring you a little mussel once in a while if that will make you happy. But don't take it so seriously. Do you think a drake really considers his words very carefully during courtship?"

"Get out!" she screamed. ""I don't want my kids to see their irresponsible father."

"Well, okay. I don't really care to see those bald kids anyway," he said. "And you're not so attractive now either, skinny as you are and full of bald spots. You're certainly not the beauty that I fell in love with."

She wanted to rush up from the nest and thrash him, but remained sitting as though she was nailed down, because now staring at her was a human being, a man, who had stuck his head up over the edge of the fjeld. Her mate fled with a loud scream, as did her aunt.

Chapter 3

But the man wasn't looking at them. He had climbed right up the fjeld and placed a large basket he had with him next to the nest.

"What a lovely nest," he said. "There's enough down feathers here for a little pillow."

"What do you want from me?" inquired the expectant mother.

"I'm not going to hurt you," said the man, "that would be just dumb of me. I put this birdhouse here purposely for you. I just want the down feathers in your nest."

"Never!" she screamed spreading her wings and hunkering down on top of the nest as quickly as she could. "What am I supposed to do about my babies?"

"Just pull out more down from your lovely breast, my little friend," said the man calmly. "Now move, so that I can reach in and get the down without any nonsense from you. I'm much the stronger, and the nest box is mine."

But the young expectant mother wouldn't budge from the spot. She pecked at his hands with her beak, screaming: "Go down to the beach and grab your down from my mate and from my old aunt! Kill them if you want and pluck out all their down; they're not worth a damn anyway. But leave my down alone."

"You're just overly excited, Little Ducky!" said the man. "The finest down comes from a mother taking it from her own breast. Everyone knows that. And if that's not so good for your babies, it's very good for others' babies... small babies of respectable families whose parents are rich enough to buy them the most splendid pillows."

"Wait at least until my babies are done with the nest!" screamed the desperate mother.

"Yeah, sure," said the man. "I'm supposed to let you sit here and scatter the down? Be gone and be quick about it."

He then pushed her aside, scooped up all the down, and put it into his basket, and left saying: "Pluck some more down from your breast if your babies need it. That's what a good mother does everywhere in the world."

She rushed to the edge of the fjeld and looked out.

Down at the beach, the eider ducks were having a romp. She could clearly see her mate and her aunt diving and enjoying themselves as though life for them was just a bowl of cherries. And the others were carrying on too, not a single one of them thinking that up here a man had come and emptied all the nests of their precious down.

"Come back here and pluck out your down feathers!" she screamed. "The time has come for you to keep a few of your promises. Your eggs are unprotected and cold even as you are frolicking down there, you good-for-nothing mate."

But her voice trailed away in the racket that the wind and the ocean breakers made. No one heard her screams and no one saw her despair. She realized that the eggs were getting really quite cold as she was standing there, and so she hurried back to the nest.

One of the eggs was beginning to crack—a little bit of a beak was peeking out from the hole in the shell. Instantly, she rushed to it and assisted the baby bird in getting out. For a moment she stood looking at it, sweet as it was. Then feverishly, she pulled out the remaining down in her breast and abdomen, stuffing them around the youngster. She quit complaining, thinking only of how to make it cozy and comfortable for her babies.

A couple of days later, all the five babies had hatched out of the eggs.

The young mother looked with pride at how lovely they were. They were already stretching their legs which had wonderful webbing between their toes; they yawned, flapped their wings and even quacked a bit.

"You all need to walk down to the beach," she said. "I'm sure that there aren't prettier ducklings anywhere on the fjeld. But if you meet up with your beastly father, just look the other way."

She began walking down and across the fjeld and the five ducklings followed her so nicely that it was a pleasure to see. Halfway down, she met the aunt.

"I was just on my way up to see you,"" said the old eider duck. "My, you have five lovely kids!"

"Yes, don't you think so?" said the mother, completely forgetting how insulted she actually was of the aunt's praises.

"Let me have one of them to walk with," asked the aunt.

"Not a chance!" said the mother fiercely. "I'm aware of how you rattle on, little aunt. My kids are mine, no one else's, and they'll stay with me."

* * *

At just that moment, a sharp crack was heard from above. It was a senseless, random firing by a dumb boy who was showing off his father's shotgun. But the shotgun was loaded, the shot scattered everywhere, and the new mother fell to the ground with a scream.

"My babies, my babies!" she groaned.

"All five of them are fine," said the aunt. "Relax now, but is there something wrong with you?"

"I am dying," said the mother. "I'm full of buckshot, and I know that I'm dying. Oh, my babies! My poor babies!"

"Don't worry about them," said the aunt. "I can take a mother's place and care for them as though they were my own."

"Ohh, aunt," said the mother in a feeble voice. "You're so awfully irresponsible. I've sat up there myself watching you frolic and dilly-dally among all the fellows and the young flirts down there. How can a mother entrust her children to you?"

"Where else will you turn to?" said the aunt. "It's quite a different story when one has kids. Lie still now until you die."

And the young mother waited to die.

She collapsed, barely seeing her babies for the last time. But the aunt didn't even wait until she was actually dead. She forgot everything except that she suddenly had inherited five, smart little ducklings, and marched them down to the beach. She knew the shortest route because she had walked it seven times before with her own offspring in tow. She prepared the paths for them, and in every way showed them how to behave correctly, stroked them with her beak, praised them, scolded them, all accordingly as they deserved it.

When their mother closed her eyes for the last time, her ducklings were already down at the beach.

They swam out quickly, ducking their heads so it was fun to see. The aunt watched over them, nearly bursting with pride.

An old cavalier came over to her and wanted to take her on a walk, but she gave him a good peck with her beak.

"Doesn't he see that I've got kids now, the old creep!" she said. "Let him get lost, or I'll teach him a lesson."

And she stayed with the young ones until they could take care of themselves. She journeyed with them south, winter after winter, hearing how the drakes proposed to them, fooling them for all the world just like their own father had done to their mother. She showed them good nesting sites, made her rounds of the couples, and was respected and looked up to by the entire fjeld until one day a white-tailed eagle took her in a flash, and ate her.

The Weeds

It was a lovely, bountiful year. Rain and sunshine alternated through the growing season in a way that was just right for the crops. As soon as the farmer began to think that it was getting a bit too dry, sure enough, it rained the next day. And when he felt that it had now rained enough, the clouds went away at once, just as though he could tell them what to do.

Clearly, the farmer was in a good mood and was able to stop complaining all the time. Cheerfully, and pleased with himself, he walked into one of his fields with his two sons.

"A great harvest is in the works this year, boys," he announced. "The barn will be full of grain, and lots of money will be coming in.

And, Jens and Olly, you'll be getting new overalls, which you can showoff when we go to the marketplace."

Meanwhile, in the grain field, the yellowing rye looked thick and heavy.

"You better start cutting me now, farmer, or I'll be too far gone and start collapsing," said the rye as it lowered its heavy spikes right down to the ground.

The farmer could see what the rye was indicating, so he hurried home to fetch his scythe.

"It's good to be at the service of folks," said the rye. "I can be sure that all of my grain kernels are taken care of," it added, knowing that most of them would be ground into flour at the miller's and then transformed into delicious tasting, fresh-baked bread, a truly noble sacrifice. The remaining kernels would be saved by the farmer for sowing next year in another field.

Nearby at the fence and the edge of the ditch bordering the field, there were a bunch of weeds, including: thistles, burdock, poppies, harebells and dandelions that were growing in tight clusters, and had heads that were chock-full of seeds. For them, too, it had been a fruitful year, naturally, as both the sunshine and the rains also provided for these insignificant plants along with the more dignified grains.

"None of us are harvested and brought into the barn," said the dandelion, shaking its head carefully so that its seeds wouldn't be released too early. "What's going to happen to all of our progeny?"

"I get a headache just thinking about it," replied the poppy. "Here I am with many hundreds of seeds in my head, ready to release them without an inkling of where to send them."

"Let's ask the rye for some advice," said the burdocks. So, they asked the rye what to do.

"When you have nothing to worry about, don't meddle in other's business," replied the rye. "But let me warn you about one thing: Watch out that you don't spill your stupid seeds over onto my field, or else you'll have me to deal with."

That warning was of no use to the wild flowers; they remained all day long speculating what to do next. At sundown, they closed their leaves in order to sleep, but kept dreaming about their seeds, and by next morning, they had it figured out.

The poppy woke up first. It carefully opened its small vaults way up at the top of its head in order that the sun could shine right onto its seeds. Then, it called upon the morning breeze that was running and playing along the fence, bordering the field. "Gentle wind," it said in a friendly tone: "Will you do me a favor?"

"Okay." answered the wind. "I don't have anything against keeping busy."

"It's just a trifling favor," added the poppy. "I beg you to just give a strong shaking to my stem, so my seeds will fly away from my vaults."

"As you wish," said the wind.

The poppy seeds flew out in all directions; the stems totally collapsed, but that was of no concern to the poppy. "If you've done all you can for your progeny, then there really isn't anything more left for you to do in this world," it sighed.

"Goodbye," said the wind, wanting only to move on.

"Wait a second," replied the poppy promptly. "Promise me first that you'll keep this action to yourself, otherwise the other weeds will get the same idea, and there will be poorer space for my seeds to flourish."

"I'm as silent as the grave is," replied the wind, and left.

"Psst! Psst!" said the harebell. "Do you have a minute to do me a tilittle favor?"

"Oh, what now!" responded the wind.

"Well, I only beg you to blow down a little upon me; I've opened up some vaults in my head and want to get my seeds well scattered to the winds, out into the world. But, please don't tell the others anything about this, or they'll get the same idea."

"Can you believe this!" said the wind, laughing. "I'll be as quiet as a mouse."

The wind proceeded to blow hard on the harebell flowers and rushed away.

"Little wind, little wind!" screamed the dandelion. "Where are you rushing to?"

"Something the matter with you, too?" inquired the wind.

"Nothing at all," replied the dandelion. "I'd just like to have a few words with you."

"Hurry up, then," said the wind. "I'm really ready to quit for the day."

"Understand, it's been a very difficult year for us to get our seeds finished and ready to disperse, and of course, we want to do the best we can for them. I don't have any notion of how it's going for the poppy and the poor burdock, but the thistle and I have put our heads together and come up with a plan. But, we need your help."

"That will be four of them," realized the wind, which made it laugh out loud.

"What are you laughing about?" asked a dandelion. "I did notice you whispering before with the harebell and the poppy, but if you mention any of this to them, we won't tell you a thing."

"Heavens!" replied the wind. "I'm as dumbstruck as a fish. What did you want?"

"We have attached a little, delicate parachute to the top of our seeds, the most delightful little toy-like thing you could imagine. If you just lightly blow on us, they can fly out into the air with their parachutes, and land as you like. How about it?"

"Okay," said the wind.

Whish! The wind rushed towards the thistle and the dandelion, releasing their seeds, and transporting them over to the field.

The burdock was still wondering when it's turn would come. It was top-heavy and thick, which is why it took so long.

But that night, a hare jumped over the fence.

"Hide me! Save me!" yelled the hare. "The farmer's dog, Prince, is after me."

"You can crawl behind the fence," said the burdock, "and I will give you cover."

"You don't seem to be able to provide that kind of assistance," said the hare, "but when it's critical, you do the best you can."

So, the hare hid behind the fence.

"In return you could carry some of my seeds over to the field," announced the burdock breaking off some of its seed-bearing heads that fell onto the fur of the hare.

Soon, Prince came trotting up to the gate. "That's the dog!" whispered the burdock, and in one leap, the hare was over the fence and into the rye field.

"Have you seen the hare, burdock?" Prince asked. "It's for sure that I've gotten too old for hunting. One eye is blind, and my nose doesn't pick up a scent anymore."

"I've seen the hare," replied the burdock, "and if you'll do me a favor, I'll show you where the hare is."

Certain of Prince's help, the burdock stuck some seed heads on the dog's back, saying to him: "If you'll just rub yourself against the small stone steps leading into the field, then my seeds will fall off from you. But that's not where you should search for the hare; I saw it recently run into the woods."

Prince carried the seeds over to the field and trotted towards the woods.

Laughing to itself, the burdock said: "Now I got my seeds transported, but God only knows how thistle, dandelion, harebell and poppy will manage it."

*   *   *

Next spring, the rye was already tall in the field.

"We are doing well, basically," said the rye plants. "We are all here, keeping each other company, amidst our own good family members. And we aren't bothering each other in the least. It's really comforting to be in the service of folks."

But one lovely day, a bunch of small poppies, and thistles, harebells and burdocks stuck their heads above the ground in the middle of the rye field.

"What's this all about," the rye demanded. "How on earth did you all arrive here?"

The poppy looked at the harebell, inquiring: "How did you get here?"

The thistle looked at burdocks: "And how on earth did you get here?"

They were all equally confused, and it took a while before they figured it out. The rye was the angriest, and when it got the picture of how each one of them received help from the hare, Prince, and the wind, it began to shout and rave.

"Thank God... the farmer shot the hare in the fall," it said. "Prince is fortunately also dead, the old scoundrel. So, those will leave me alone now. But how dare the wind deliver those weed seeds over to the farmer's field."

"Not so furious... you upstart rye!" ordered the wind, waiting behind the fence and hearing everything discussed. "I don't ask anyone for permission, but do what pleases me, and now I demand that you bow to me."

Then, the wind blew strongly over the young rye plant so that the thin stalk swayed back and forth.

"Now see here... the farmer cultivates his rye, because that's his livelihood. The sun and I, we busy ourselves with all of you without regard to your standing. For us, the lowly weed is just as pretty as the more respected rye."

The farmer came out to his field to inspect his rye, and when he saw the weeds growing in it, he scratched his head with annoyance, and started to curse.

"That dirty, rotten wind," he said to Jens and Olly standing next to him with hands in the pockets of their new overalls.

But the wind blew harder, knocking off their three caps and tossing them far along the path. The farmer and both boys ran after them, but the wind was faster. Finally, the caps rolled into the village pond, and the farmer and the boys had to take a long time fishing them out before they managed to get them back.

The Eel's Unlucky Day

*O*ut over the ocean, the sea gulls flew as far as their wings could carry them, and ships sailed to wherever people navigated them. Sometimes it was calm; sometimes it was stormy. Sometimes a sailor fell overboard and drowned; sometimes a ship capsized taking man and mouse, and you never heard of it again.

Down in the depths, far under the sea gulls and the ships, the flounder was bored to tears, its mouth all twisted.

"It would be nice if something was happening," said the flounder. "It's lovely enough here in the seaweed stand, and it's also cool, quiet, and safe. But sometimes I would so much like to see what the rest of the world looks like."

"The world is the same everywhere," said the herring. "Water and seaweed, seaweed and water, mussels, creeping snails, and flounders with twisted mouths. It's six of one and half a dozen of the other. I'm sure of this because I swim out every year through the Little Belt, and back home through the Great Belt."

"Do you call that a trip?" said the cod scornfully. "Well, I take a trip every year out to the Atlantic Ocean, which is quite something else. But you are right; the world is the same everywhere."

"I don't think so," said the flounder. "Something in me says that you're all wrong."

"You ought to have your eyes put straight in your head," said the cod. "The way you're oriented, you only get to see about half of what an ordinary codfish sees. That's probably why you're so dissatisfied."

"Goodness gracious, how you fellows talk," said the oyster. "Isn't everything just fine as it is? What do we care about the boring world? In my youth, I traveled around just like you've done, and it wasn't fun at all. Now I'm quite settled down, permanently anchored, and thank heaven every day for fresh water, good food, and peaceful days."

There wasn't anything else to say on that score, so they were all quiet.

Then the eel arrived.

"Here comes the eel," said the cod. "It must be fall."

"Where were you this summer?" asked the flounder.

"Hello there," said the eel. "I have been to a lake."

"Heavens," said the cod. "How did you manage to breathe in that water? If I even get near the beach at the river's mouth, I'm ready to suffocate."

"Oh," said the eel, "it's no good always expecting so much. You have to wiggle a bit."

"If only I could wiggle," said the flounder sighing.

"I can't comprehend why you guys want to run around so much," said the oyster. "Why are you here now, eel?"

"My young are born here," said the eel. "Also, I prefer the ocean in the winter. It's deeper, not so cold, and with much less ice. But as soon as it's spring, I'm off again. It's fresh water time for me!"

"Do you take your kids with you?" asked the cod. "I don't recall ever seeing a young eel."

"They're really not so easy to spot," said the eel. "To start with, they're nothing but a little piece of thread, but exceptionally agile. They make their way up the lake by themselves, and I give them only one rule to live by."

"Does one dare ask what that could be?" inquired the herring.

"I simply tell them they have to wiggle,'" said the eel, and then it swam away.

"That is quite irresponsible advice for a father to give," said the oyster. "My young ones wiggle too, but if I could, I'd rather teach them to grab on to something rigid right away."

*   *   *

When spring came, the eel was back in the lake.

"Spring must be coming," said the perch. "There's the eel."

"Welcome back," said the sunfish. "Where have you been this winter?"

"Hello there everyone," said the eel; "is the pike around?"

"It's at the other end of the lake," said the sunfish, "but it could be here any moment, and then all hell is going to break loose."

"Oh, so what?" said the eel, "you just have to wiggle. But to answer your question, sunfish, I'm been in the ocean; that's where I had my young again."

"Ah," said the perch, "I think maybe I ate a couple of them at lunch time...oh, excuse me for blurting it right out."

"It's okay," replied the eel; "even so, the family is big enough."

"How in the world did they get up here from the ocean?" asked the sunfish.

"I'm pretty sure just like I had to do myself, right after I was born. First, I swam up the river as long as it reached, and then I sailed down a brook until it ran out."

"And then what?" asked the perch.

"Well...," said the eel. "I then wiggled myself through a wonderfully wet meadow, right at the base of the grasses where the sunshine couldn't get to me, and where it was quite moist. It wasn't exactly pleasant, but it went well enough."

"What a life for a fish!" said the perch.

"Psst! It's the pike!" yelled the sunfish.

Stretching out its fins, it swam for dear life, and the perch did the same.

"You have to wiggle," said the eel.

And one, two, three... it was down in the mud again.

*　　*　　*

As fall approached, the eel was on its way to the ocean. Though the grass wasn't nearly as tall as in the spring, the eel was in the middle of its journey through the meadow when two large boys on their way home spotted it crawling.

"What a disgusting grass snake," said one of the boys thrashing it over the back with his stick.

"Ouch," said the eel.

"That's not a grass snake, it's an eel." said the other boy.

"Ouch," said the eel, again.

Both boys rushed over to the eel and grabbed one end of the eel each, and no matter how much it twisted and squirmed, it didn't help; it couldn't wiggle any more. The boys held it with both their hands and lifted it up into the air.

"What a fellow!" said one of the boys.

They walked off carefully sideways with it, but after moving just a bit, the eel slipped from their hands.

"There he goes, the sneaky beast," said one of the boys.

"You have to wiggle," said the eel.

"After him!" said the other boy.

Quickly they captured it again, and this time they stuffed it into one of the boys' cap and took care to keep an eye on it.

"That's really quite an eel," said their mother when they brought it home.

She then called to the kitchen girl, Sally.

"It's best if Sally skins it immediately," she said, "because an eel is so lively; it can travel on land as much as it can swim in the water."

Sally grabbed the eel with her rough, left hand, and in her right hand she wielded a sharp knife. Swish! She cut a long line right across the belly of the eel, and it reacted so violently that she became frightened, and the eel slipped from her hand. In a flash, the eel wiggled itself across the kitchen floor.

"You slippery, disgusting beast!" Sally screamed, and ran after it with the knife still in her hand.

"You have to wiggle," said the eel, but the boys caught it again.

"Let's put it right into the frying pan," said the mother, "or it will never give up."

Sally put the frying pan on the stove and added some butter. She then took hold of the eel, finished skinning it, cut its head off, and dipped it in flour.

She then put it into the pan, as the fire crackled, and the butter sizzled.

"Can you believe it, this fellow is still wiggling," said Sally.

"You need to wigg…"

The eel said no more, because then it died.

The Little Herring

Chapter 1

High on the north coast of Norway, a little fishing village nestles at the base of a wide mountain, which the locals call a **fjord** that leads into a large expanse of ocean. The houses are small, simple, and built of wood. There is a little church, also made of wood, but without a steeple. The grocer and the doctor have houses, too, and there's an old, low-lying rectory. Down at the beach, the boats are usually dragged up onto the sand to avoid being washed out to sea.

The village's residents are mostly fishermen, and if the fish don't come on time in a given year, then there is great anxiety, everyone fearing the worst. Now in the year that this story begins, they had waited a long time for the **herring run**, which is what they call it when the herring swarm out in the wide ocean.

"If the herring don't come, we'll all die," said the oldest fisherman's wife. "I've lived for seventy-two years, and it's never happened yet that the summer herring haven't arrived by this late date in August. None of us have a scrap of bread left in the house."

The grocer paced around looking dejectedly at the many, many barrels of salt he had purchased to preserve them until they could be sold. He looked up in his account book to see how many loans he had extended to the fishermen and became even more dejected.

"If the herring don't come, I'll go bust," he said.

"If the herring don't come, we're leaving for America," said the young fishermen.

"If the herring don't come, it's because you're all sinners," said the minister.

"If the herring don't come this year, it's because the ocean isn't salty enough," said the doctor. "Or, because the water isn't warm enough. Or, because the bottom of the sea isn't a good place for their eggs."

They all listened to these varied opinions shaking their heads. Most of them feared the minister might be right and the doctor wrong. But then there was an older fisherman, Olly, who seldom said anything, and for this reason they listened to him attentively.

"I'm going to tell you something, youngsters," he squeezed in. "If the herring aren't running, it's because the whales, the gulls, and the cod aren't chasing them in."

"You're such a fool, Olly," said the doctor. "The whales, the gulls, and the cod—they chase after the herring exactly like you do. Wherever you think the herring are, that's where you'd expect them to be."

"Sure, when the doctor can tell me where the herring are, I'm ready to go there," said Olly. "As far as I can tell, the herring and I are in different places right now."

Everybody, including the doctor, laughed, and Olly realized he was spouting off.

"Mind what I tell you," he said. "As soon as you see the whales and the gulls out there, then you can expect the herring to start running immediately."

They all climbed up the path to the top of the mountain and gazed out at the ocean. They saw nothing that day, or the day after that, and so the days went by.

"Let's pray to God for Him to forgive us our sins," said the minister.

"Let's pray to God that He makes the water turn warm and salty, and the sea bottoms just like the herring want it," said the doctor.

"Let's pray to God that He gets the whales and the gulls out chasing after the herring," said Olly the fisherman.

Some of them prayed, some of them cursed and scolded, and some of them cried and carried on, each according to his nature. But every day, any living creature that could crawl and walk climbed up the mountain and looked out over the ocean.

Chapter 2

One day old Olly was standing up on the highest mountain with his large binoculars when he let out a hefty yell.

"It's them"! he screamed.

"Can you see them from that distance, Olly?" the doctor asked.

"No, but I can see the whale," said Olly. "It's spraying out a huge fan of water from its blowholes. It's like a fountain way up in the air, and I can count ten squirts in a huge arch that stretches over the beach. You all can do what you want, but I'm going down to attend to my nets."

"Wait a minute," said the doctor. "There's no reason to be in such a rush, Olly. If the herring are here, you know well enough that they'll remain here until they've completed laying their eggs. Since each of them needs to lay at least thirty-thousand eggs, we don't need to rush."

Now all of them could see the whales out in the ocean sending their water spray up into the air. More and more of them crowded together in an enormous circle as far as the eyes could see. They could also see the whales' large backs, and the dolphins and the tuna were also leaping in the air, and above them the noisy gulls were flying in ever tighter flocks. Every other one of them skimmed the water and picked up a herring that had ventured too close to the surface.

"Oh yes, there they are," admitted the doctor.

"That's where they are," said Olly, pointing out to the sea.

Everyone looked where Olly was pointing and could see how the water had become strangely smooth, bright, and shining with unusual colors. It was the herring amassing in **shoals** under the surface of the ocean. Thousands and thousands of fish—or maybe there were many more—whose bubbles kept constantly rising up to the water's surface before they burst.

"The herring are swarming higher up on the water this year," said Olly.

"How so?" asked the doctor.

"Well, because, the air bubbles aren't bursting, you see," explained Olly. "If the bubbles did burst at the same time they were ascending, then the herring would be further down. "You see," continued Olly, "the dissolved oxygen the herring take in down below is under a lot more pressure than that nearer the surface, so the deeper the fish are swimming, absorbing the oxygen from the water through their gills, the more the bubbles will burst on coming up to the surface where the pressure of the air is much reduced. Didn't they teach that to you at school?"

"There's got to be an enormous number of herring out there," said the minister, a bit embarrassed.

"That there is," said Olly. "We also call it **Herring Mountain**."

"How big is that mountain, Olly?" asked the doctor.

"You can judge for yourself, doctor," said Olly. "It easily goes for a couple of miles on one side, and a couple of miles on the other side. And it wouldn't surprise me if it went down thirty feet. Maybe the good doctor can figure out for me how many herring that amounts to."

The doctor was calculating.

"I figure there'll be about five-hundred million," he then said.

"No, I don't think so," said Olly with certainty in his voice.

"Then we'd all be drowning in herring," said the minister.

"Nonsense," said the doctor. "Look at how the gulls, the whales, and the sharks feed. No one sees what the cod get underneath the water; they are the most ravenous of all. There'll be less than one percent of all those herrings salted down in the grocer's barrels."

"Yes, but more will come of course," said the minister. "The doctor's estimate was right on target. I thought you said that every herring laid thirty-thousand eggs. How many of them will make it to adulthood?"

"Two," said the doctor.

"Two thousand?" said the minister.

"Two," repeated the doctor.

"No, I don't think that can be right," said the minister.

Chapter 3

Then they all marched down the mountain, pushed their boats out to sea, and began the herring catch. The haul was better than any other year they could remember. The nets that they reeled in were so full that the boats almost capsized. The women worked from morning until night picking the fish out of the nets. The entire village shone like silver from all the herring scales. Everywhere you looked, you only saw or smelled herring. But that was only for the good; herring meant food, clothing, and happy times.

Steamships arrived just to fetch the many thousands of barrels of salted herring. The grocer used up all the salt that he had and had to send for even more. The fishermen paid up their debts to him, and purchased brandy, tobacco, and twine for their new nets, pork for the winter, a new scarf for the wife, and anything else the lady's heart desired.

The herring haul lasted for over a month, and when it ended, everyone was happy and content.

"God forgave you your sins," said the minister.

"The water was suitably warm and salty, and the bottom was fine," said the doctor.

"The whales and the gulls came at the right time," said Olly.

$$* \quad * \quad *$$

Meanwhile, the grocer up in the fishing village was counting all the money he had earned, and while all the village folks were congratulating themselves on the fine herring haul, the herring that had managed to escape with their lives, were on their way back out to sea again.

But they had laid their eggs at the bottom of the fjord before leaving. They were extremely small eggs, glued together forming strings, and attached to rocks, seaweed, and about anything lying on the fjord bottom. There were so many of them that it would be simply impossible to count them. A large number of them were consumed by small animals swimming around down there. But there were still plenty of eggs lying in the clear, quiet waters waiting to be hatched.

And eventually the larvae emerged. They were an odd appearing fish, no mouth, but with two large eyes, and a large yolk sac from the egg, still hanging from their abdomen. They were transparent, had no scales, and it wouldn't occur to anyone that they would ever grow into herring.

Gradually, as they came out of the eggs, they swam away. Finally, there weren't more than two eggs remaining. They were attached together on a stone, sitting there for over a month, without any idea at all of what was going to happen to them.

"Aren't you feeling something?" said one of the eggs.

"Yes, I am," said the other egg. "Something is pulling at me—it won't be long now."

"It's about time, said the first egg. All the others are gone, and we're sitting here all on our own."

"That's because we are at the deepest level," said the second egg. "It's quite cold here, and that's why it has taken us so long."

So, they waited some more, sitting close to each other until a hole appeared out of which swam the two herring larvae that resembled the others except that they were larger for having incubated so much longer.

"What now?" said the first larva.

"Yes, what now?" said the second larva.

They peered into the clear water as far as they could see with their large eyes. They saw cod gliding by, and other strange animals they were afraid of. They didn't know what route to take and kept close together exactly like when they were still in the eggs.

"I don't think life is very easy for a young herring," said one of the larvae.

"Okay, but we'll stick together," said the other larva. "We're sisters and we'll never desert one another."

"Well, it's possible that we'll get separated from each other," said the number one larva. "I think it's terrible the way the waves roll in."

"That could happen," said number two larva. "But in that case, we'll just meet somewhere else in the world."

"Do you think we'll recognize each other by then?" said the number one larva. "All the herring in the world are identical; that's what our mother said when she deposited me."

"Yes, she did say that," replied number two larva. "Gee, do you remember everything that mother said? She told us about her long journeys, all the fears she had, and the dangers she faced. She spoke of the nasty seagulls, the sharks and whales, and all the other animals that had given her chase, and even some that went chasing after her newborns. She mentioned people that intercepted the herring shoal and caught them in nets."

"Yes, but that doesn't happen to us until we're grown up," said the number one larva.

"Don't you also remember the things she told us about all the animals who wanted to eat us when we were small. I've already realized that what mother told us is right. I saw many, many of our sisters being consumed right after being released from the egg."

"Sure, there were certainly lots of them eaten even when they were still in the egg," said the number one larva.

"Yes, then let's stick together," said the number two larva. "If only there were more of us. The ocean is mighty huge for two small herring to be facing it alone."

"When we venture out, we'll probably find someone to go with," said the number one larva.

They began to swim out into the ocean as best they could. But they were so small, and so weak that as soon as they had swum only a mile from land, they had the idea that they were already out into the deep ocean. Then they bumped into other herring and followed along. And while swimming along, eating whatever they could find, they grew to maturity resembling a typical herring. They had gotten mouths just a few days after coming out of the eggs. They were no longer transparent, now had grown fins, and had quite small, silvery-glistening scales.

Chapter 4

But the two who had shared the same place on the rock as eggs stuck together the whole time.

"Let's go up" said the number one herring. "I'd like to go up to the surface. It's so delightfully light there."

They both swam up but scurried down again as the glare of the light cut into their eyes, and from then on, they never surfaced again except in the darkness of night.

"Where do we actually swim then?" said the number two herring.

"I'm going to follow that cloud which is in front of me in the water," said the number one herring. "That's a ***food-cloud*** which you can certainly see, and I really don't want to do anything else but eat until I've grown up to be really big, strong and husky."

They swam after the cloud which was an enormously large collection of tiny, almost invisible animals flitting here and there as the wind and the sea's current moved them.

The doctor up in the fishing village called the cloud **plankton**, and told the minister and Olly about them, just as he had observed them under his microscope. "They're the herring's favorite food," he said.

But Olly wouldn't believe him.

"Herring live off water," Olly said. "No one has ever found anything except water in a herring's stomach."

"Watch out for that cod over there!" said the number one herring, bolting as quickly as lightning to the bottom.

"Where ...?" said the number two herring just as the cod roared by with an open mouth and swallowed it.

✳   ✳   ✳

The little herring was now left alone. She had enough friends, because just like everything else that grows and thrives, the shoal of herring also flourished and consisted already of many thousands of fish. But she was missing the one that had been her friend right from start and mentioned this to the other herring.

"A little herring doesn't do well to be alone," she said.

But suddenly a large, fat old herring appeared unexpectedly among all the young fish.

"A herring that is alone is no herring," said the old fish. "Only when the herring band together into a huge mountain of herring, do they have any hope of garnering respect. Then the sharks, the whales, the cod and the gulls prey on us. Also, people. And those who make it through all that, neither caught nor eaten, have some hope of laying their eggs, slipping away and reassembling into a new shoal to begin life all over again."

"It's a rotten life," said the little herring.

"Life is never good," said the old herring. "Cod hunt herring, sharks hunt cod, and people hunt sharks."

"Who hunts people?" asked the little herring.

"I don't know," said the old herring. "A little herring can ask more questions than ten old herring have answers for. But be assured, people have their enemies, too, just like us."

They then swam away, and as the days passed, the shoal grew larger.

Soon the shoal was heading out toward the ocean, eating... always eating... the plankton swarm that was bobbing in the water everywhere like a cloud. Soon, the shoal was feeding under the coastal edge as the cloud of plankton drifted there.

But after six months of this routine, the little herring thought she had grown up enough, so she could now do something else than eat all the time.

"Food just doesn't taste that good to me anymore," she said.

"That's just because you're always so filled up," said the old herring. "I suppose that you're now grown up enough so you're ready to lay eggs."

"Where shall I lay them?" asked the now grown-up herring.

"You need to lay them up in the fjord in the same place where you were born," said the old herring. "You know I've been there five times, so I'm familiar with that place. But we don't venture up there until we are forced to. That's a life-threatening trip that you don't take, just for the fun of it."

They swam, and they swam. Then an enormous storm suddenly came up.

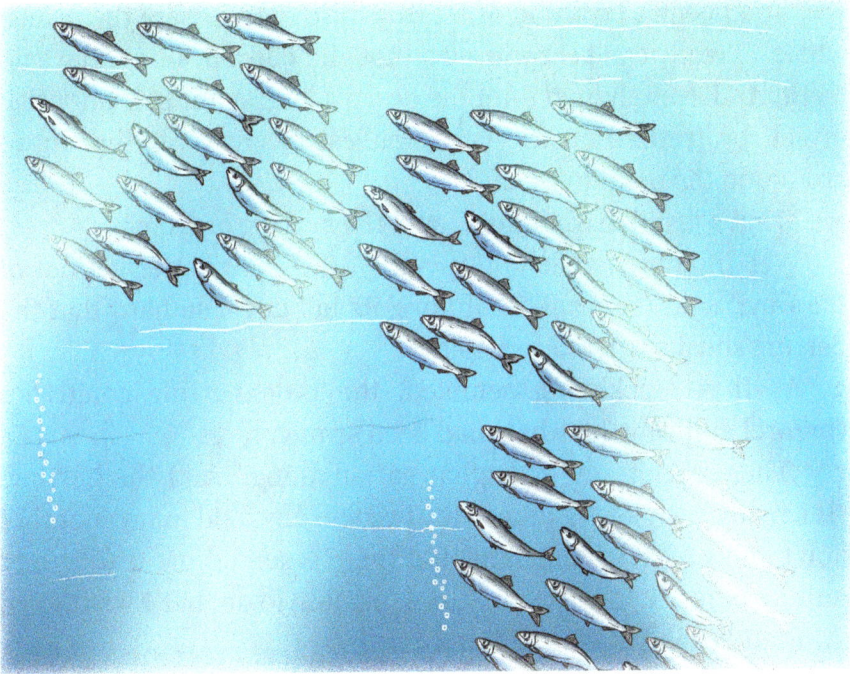

"Race to the bottom, race to the bottom, and swim out to the ocean," yelled the old herring. "Close ranks around me. I'm the strongest and will take the lead and the largest of you—follow behind me as close to each other as you can, side by side, mouth to tail. We need to be like one enormous fish breaking cleanly through the water."

They did as the old herring demanded, and the whole shoal scurried out to the ocean. They kept close to the bottom as long as the storm lasted. But when it was peaceful again, and they ascended, they saw an enormously large baleen whale lying perfectly still on the water's surface.

A terrible commotion commenced. The little herring quivered right in front of the whale's mouth, paralyzed from sheer fright.

"You needn't be afraid of me, my little friend," said the baleen whale. "I really can't eat you even though I'd like to since I have no teeth. And even though I am the ocean's largest animal, I nourish myself by feeding on the very smallest of creatures that move around in the plankton-cloud."

"That's just like what I do," said the herring joyfully.

Well, if you encroach on my prey, then you better get out of the way," said the whale slamming its tail down so hard that the herring shoal scattered to all sides.

As they quickly reassembled, the little herring could not comprehend why the whale had been so angry.

"There aren't any of us that eat anything," said the herring. "It's really been a long time since I've had any food in my mouth. I don't know what's happening, but there is something tearing and pulling in me. I don't know what I'm going to do, but I want to go away and experience something."

"What you want is to lay your eggs," said the old herring. "That's what we all want to do. Let's get going. Youngsters, line up, and let's swim away to the fjord."

New herring came from everywhere to join the shoal that was almost two miles long and just as wide. The ocean was churning and roaring as it moved.

From high up in the air, the screaming sea gulls descended. As soon as a herring got too near the surface, the white bird flew down, grabbed it, and ate it at once.

"It's good to be far down," said the little herring pressing herself in among the other herring.

At the same moment, there was a terrific jolt and shockwave sideways in the water. It was a huge cod rushing through the shoal grabbing one herring after the other with its sharp teeth and swallowing them.

"Well, this isn't silly game stuff, "said the old herring. "Perhaps you'd like to consider leaving the shoal now?"

"No, no, I need to swim ahead," said the herring. "I just feel it in me that I can't turn back."

"Well, you're right about that," said the old herring. "You really couldn't do it if you wanted. If you're courageous enough to stick your nose up to the surface, you'll see for yourself."

The herring did just that but retreated rapidly down again.

The whole sky was full of screaming gulls, and all around as far as she could see, dolphins and tuna were jumping, and the large whales were sending water sprays high up into the air.

"We're completely encircled," said the herring terrified.

"We are indeed", said the old herring. "Now look in toward the shore—there are all these people ready with their nets and boats, and those horrible salt barrels that we get stuffed into if we don't manage to escape."

"I need to swim on anyway," said the herring. "I don't know why, but I must go forward."

"That's determined by nature," said the old herring, "and no one can defy nature that doesn't care whether you are big or little. There is no animal in the world so large that it can defy its own destiny. Onward herrings—forward, forward."

And advance they did with unstoppable power.

The cod ate them, the gulls grabbed them, but the masses of them reassembled again, and it seemed like there were just as many of them regardless of how many were eaten. None of them thought anymore about their fellow traveler, but only kept swimming steadily in, headed toward the fjord.

$$* \quad * \quad *$$

"It's going to be a fantastic herring catch again this year," said Olly standing on the mountain looking out.

"Yes, it's a happy coastline," said the doctor.

"God blesses us despite all our sins," said the minister.

They then all ran down the mountain, set their boats loose, threw their nets out, and dragged in one heavy haul after the other.

But the little herring was now treading in the deep water near the bottom, not thinking at all about the dangers she was exposed to, but just depositing her eggs, first ten, then twenty, then a hundred, a thousand, until she was relieved of them all.

And as she was depositing the eggs, she talked just like her mother talked in her time—totally confused in the water, and not worrying at all who heard her:

"Oh, little ones, little ones, it's a joy to live, and a joy to swim in the large ocean. The gulls are after us, sharks, cod, tuna, people, and many other vicious animals. But nothing in the world can compare to the life of a herring. Oh, you don't know how wonderful it is to swim behind a cloud of plankton, eating day and night. You don't know how beautiful and peaceful it is down in the deep water with the waves rolling above us. You don't know how incredible it is to come up to the surface in the still and darkness of night sparkling with your scales in the dim light."

"But nothing was really as wonderful as the journey up here to the fjord in order to bring you into the world. I can't begin to explain it to you since I'll never be able to recognize you in life, even if I did run into you, because one herring is just like another. You won't know anything about me, and I won't know anything about you. I also know that almost none of you will make it through life. We were just two of thirty thousand brothers and sisters, and one of us was eaten before she was really developed."

"But that doesn't matter. Life is wonderful, and the herring is the ocean's happiest animal. Save yourselves, as many of you as can, and become lovely, shiny herring that sparkle in the ocean."

Having said all that, she had also finished depositing her eggs, and was so tired that she could hardly hold up any longer. She looked about her and noticed that the entire shoal was spread out. Many had been caught, many had been eaten, and many had managed to sneak away having laid their eggs. The entire bottom of the ocean was full of herring eggs.

"Yes, yes," said the once-little-herring. "Herring will come again next year; you can bet on that. But I better see if I can find something to eat now."

She swam away, and no one raised a finger to her.

The fishermen headed in with their boats and nets. The sharks and the cod went elsewhere; the gulls sat up on the coastal cliffs digesting their food.

"It's terrible how exhausted I am," said the herring. "But it's actually not so surprising that setting thirty thousand babies into the world saps my strength."

So, she swam on. Occasionally she met some old friends but didn't care to chat with them at all.

"I'm just too tired," she said.

"Well, we certainly are too," said her friends.

✳   ✳   ✳

For over three months, the herring kept to herself eating and eating. Slowly she began regaining her strength and began longing for some company. She met a herring, then another, soon more, and quickly they organized themselves into a little shoal again.

One lovely day, they met the old herring.

"Well, you also managed to escape?" said the younger herring.

"Just like you did," said the old one. 'Life is a lottery, nothing else, and a herring is the prize. This time, my number didn't come up, but the next time I might not be so lucky. What are you up to now, youngsters? Are you going to the fjord again to lay some eggs?"

"Oh, we're not in that much of a hurry," said the no-longer little herring. "Let's enjoy life a bit first, swim up and down, eat a lot, and practice swimming in a shoal again."

"Yes, let's do it," yelled the others.

And so, they all swam around, formed into a shoal, descended to the ocean bottom when it stormed, and followed after the plankton cloud wherever it drifted.

"I think I'm feeling queer again," said the once-little herring. "Food has no taste to me anymore. I'd love to be in the fjord where I was born from an egg, and where I deposited all of my own eggs last time."

"Away to the fjord," said the old herring. Align yourselves side by side, head to tail. It's egg-laying time, and we have to leave."

They all headed to the fjord.

And the gulls were there along with the sharks, the whales, the cod, the minister, the doctor, and Olly, all waiting at the beach.

But if the once-little herring was caught this time, or the next, or the next, we do not really know.

Because all herrings look the same.

The Four Cousins

Chapter 1

The judges had left, and the villa was empty. A woman had been cleaning up all the rooms, the yard swept, and everything locked up because the place was not for rent again. A rat was racing around, up the stairs to the attic, down the stairs to the cellar, sniffing everywhere, but there was nothing to find.

"Wretched people, damn ordinary people," said the rat. "Everything, gone with the wind; not so much as a morsel of anything left for a hungry rat."

He ran down to the yard, and after crawling under the door of the woodshed, he looked around. "Nothing to keep me here," he said. "I'll almost surely have to leave, too." And so, he ran away.

But he was wrong in thinking there was nothing in the woodshed. There was no food for him, for sure, but four things remained behind that would have been useful if the house had stayed open in the winter.

Each was lying in its respective corner, minding its own business. One was a pile of black and shiny coal, the second was coke resembling charcoal in clumps, looking dull and tired, and the third was cords of beech firewood, shining white in the dim light. Finally, the fourth was a miserable pile of peat. But the room wasn't so large that they couldn't chat with each other, and since there was no one else around, they ended up doing just that.

* * *

"That idiot rat," said the coal. "The simpleton saying there was nothing around, and here I am."

"Me too," said firewood. "You can't overlook me."

"Hey, don't forget me," added the coke with a faltering voice. "I can't yell like the coal and firewood because I've been through so much, which has taken its toll on me, but I'm just as worthy as the rest of you."

"Well, I'm also around... I guess," said peat modestly. "Pardon me for butting in."

Coal looked around.

"Of course, you're all here," said coal. "I don't deny it. But what good are you? That's the important thing."

"Well," said peat, "I'm only a bit of fuel. Excuse me for saying that, but you asked me."

"So am I," said coke.

"Me too," said firewood. "But I don't know if the snooty coal is good for anything but burning."

"Right," said coal. "We'd all be used for fuel if someone hadn't left us here, but just because we all ended up in the same place isn't to say we all have equal value. I'm the hottest by far; there's so much heat inside me that sometimes I'm ready to explode."

"But I'm the prettiest and most expensive," said firewood. "Only the rich can afford to burn me."

"I'm the cleanest," said coke.

"Excuse me," said peat bragging, "but I'm the cheapest."

"Heavens!" said coal. "Each of us has its advantage. But I still think no one will contradict me if I propose that I am of the finest family. I am descended from ancient times, and no one in the entire world has lived longer than me."

"Well, I have," said coke.

"What kind of nonsense is that?" responded coal.

"Well, I'm not a young squirt myself," said peat, "but I would just never talk about that subject."

"And I'm young and hearty," said firewood. "I'm not even thoroughly dried out. But you can all go to blazes with your ridiculous ages."

They were suddenly quiet for a moment, and then peat said:

"Excuse me, but shouldn't we all just tell our own stories? We will lie here for a half, maybe even a whole year, and telling stories is always so much fun."

"It's fine with me," said coke. "But I must insist that you let me speak last. First, I'm so weak that I need to pull myself together beforehand. Second, I'm nervous that you won't have patience enough to hear me out. Third..."

"I'll give you the last place as a present," said firewood. "Now let me begin. My story is fresh on my mind, and quite something. I remember it like yesterday."

"Oh, go on then," said coal. "After you, we'll hear from peat, and then I'll speak. Coke is last."

Chapter 2 — Firewood's Story

"I was once the proudest tree in the forest," said firewood.

"Braggart," said coal. "Just you wait until it's my turn."

"Quiet!" demanded firewood. "I was a huge beech tree and I stood in a magnificent forest with my branches reflecting on the glistening water of the lake. Every spring, I broke out in bud, and I can tell you I was a sight to behold. But I need not tell you that because others already have. Everyone who saw me swooned with admiration."

"I was so outstanding that a poet wrote verses about me and had them published in the newspaper. Many lovers carved their names in my bark. There were two ravens who built their nests in my crown, and all around me lived finches and starlings, delighted with the lodgings."

"It sounds lovely," said coal. "What a shame one can't see anything like that on you now."

"If we're interrupted like that," said coke, "I'm not about to tell you anything when it's my turn. Let's have respect for each other's story and be patient."

"At my trunk's base, I always had a delightful carpet," said the beech. "In the spring, white anemones popped up, followed by fine, green grass, and every summer I grew larger, adding more branches in the crown, and one more tree ring to my trunk. In the fall and the winter, I fashioned my own surroundings of my withered brown leaves, lying thick and densely packed on the surrounding ground until the snows came."

"I was a regular giant in the forest, and when it stormed most fiercely in the winter and my compatriots... weaker trees... were splitting in their trunks regularly, I came through with flying colors. I had a long and wonderful life."

"Pardon me," said peat. "But how did it end?"

"Apparently, I got too big," answered the firewood, sounding less positive than before. "I heard people talking about the need for the smaller trees to establish themselves too, and that I would provide a lot of firewood or raw materials for making furniture."

"Ah, people... Ha, Ha, Ha!" said coal knowingly.

"Yes, people! Ha, Ha! Ha! I'll stop laughing," said coke "but I shouldn't. We're all dependent on people."

"I don't know what you're all laughing about," said firewood, quite insulted. "People are our constant master, I suppose. They sliced a V-shaped piece out of my trunk, put the saw to me, wrapped a rope around me, and pulled on me until I toppled. It took thirty men to do it, and I fell with such a bang that the earth shook like an earthquake. I was then sawed up again and again, split with axes, stacked up, sold at auction, and driven to houses. Now all that's left of me is these few pieces of me in a pile. That's my story, and if any of you has a better one, be my guest."

"That's quite an unusual story," said coal, "but let's now hear from peat."

"Well, I'm sorry," said peat. "It's so trivial what I have to tell you that..."

"Tell it to us now anyway," said the others. "We've nothing else to do but listen."

Chapter 3 – Peat's Story

"I was once the proudest tree in the forest," said peat but it didn't get to say any more before they all burst out laughing. Poor peat looked more like a lump of forgotten earth.

"Oh, excuse me," said peat. "You really must excuse me; I can understand how funny it sounds, but what can I do? I have to tell my story just as it is."

"Sorry, peat," they all said. "Please carry on."

"Thank you. Well now, I really was a lovely tree even if you can't see that now. I wasn't a beech tree, for sure, but just a birch."

"The birch is a beautiful tree," said firewood, "still, not too important as a species, and it doesn't provide much shade, but it's a fine tree."

"Thanks a lot," said peat.

"I suppose people cut you down too?" inquired firewood.

"No, they didn't," replied peat. "Honestly, I never saw a human being until I eventually became peat. That's why I had to laugh before when you mentioned people, even if I were out of line."

"Get on with it," said coal.

"Yes, I'm sorry," said peat. "So, I was a birch tree. True enough, I had no birds nesting in me, but in the swamp—part of the forest where I was standing—there were birds, deer, foxes, wolves and bears. In the summer, the growling bear walked around with her cubs. In the winter, the wolves howled with hunger that was heard many miles away. There were also elk in great herds, and huge eagles flew around but, like with firewood, it all ended suddenly."

"Were you chopped up like me?" asked firewood.

"No, I wasn't. A frightful storm came up one day, toppling me, and I fell straight into the swamp. I lay there for an awfully long time, right through the first spring, and I actually budded just like when I was standing on my own roots. But that ended soon enough.

The beaver came along, gnawed on me, and because of the water, I rotted. Eventually, I broke clean free from my stump, and I sank."

"Well, well," said coal. "You really have had experiences."

"Continue," said coke.

"It was not nice at all. I sank down, of course, and I sank, and I sank. Sometimes I descended in a hurry, other times more slowly. I'd get caught up in something, and then my branches would stop me from hitting the bottom. But down I went into the murky water. On me grew all kinds of greenery, and one thing and another came down on top of me until finally I got completely buried in the muck and such. And then I really rotted."

"Ugh," said firewood. "It's so disgusting to rot. I remember once I had an injury to my side where a branch broke off. The woodpecker came and pecked out a big hole, followed by chomping larvae, and the rain formed a little pool and it was awful. I had a relative standing right next to me who had a similar experience, but it ended up becoming a hollowed-out tree."

"Let's continue hearing from peat," said coke.

"I don't have more to tell you," said peat. "Eventually, I rotted completely, and there wasn't a knot left in the middle of me. I got mixed together with everything else in the swamp, and the stuff that came down from above pushed, and pushed so hard on us, that I finally didn't know any more what belonged to me and what belonged to the others around me."

"Century after century passed until one day people came along, and they cut up everything at the bottom of the swamp into slices. I was now part of the peat, and they packed me into cakes in the field, dried me in the sun, broke me into pieces, placed me in piles, and sold me to the judge and the people who own the big houses. That's all there is. I apologize, but there's nothing more to say."

"That was something, peat," said coal, "and a lot more interesting than firewood's story. You have age in you, peat, and

that's the point. Only the old stories are worth anything. All this modern stuff is just junk."

"Well," said firewood, "I have my three hundred years to show."

"And I'm about two thousand years old," said peat.

"Let's get coal's story now," said coke.

And coal began:

Chapter 4 — Coal's Story

"I was once the proudest tree in the forest."

"Oh, you too?" said firewood laughing. "You must have been a pretty black tree."

"My dear firewood," said coal, "laugh as much as you like. Ignorant folks always laugh at what they don't understand, but I assume you'll have laughing cramps before I'm done with my story."

"Go on," said coke.

"Well, yes—it's easy for you to say, but it's harder to do. There probably isn't one of you that can comprehend even slightly what I'm about to tell you."

"Oh, I can," said coke.

"I wonder?" said coal sarcastically. "My story isn't for frayed nerves, but listen up now. It's better to tell you straight away I am from England, and when I was a tree then, there was an abundance of huge forests."

"On the journey here, I came through your woods—you know, the place where firewood stood as a beech tree and peat was a birch. I don't like talking down about anyone, especially not those lower on the species ladder than myself, but it surely was a pitiful forest then. Now, when I was a tree, we had an abundance of real forests. But it was also hundreds of thousands of years ago."

"Nonsense," scoffed firewood.

"It's true," said coke.

"I'm so glad that coke believes me," said coal, "even though it has no more reason to than firewood. None of you has seen these magnificent forests; those standing then are now gone, utterly gone. The only thing left of them resides in the coal. In contrast, both the beech and the birch are still found in forests everywhere."

"Continue," said coke.

"In such a forest, I was the proudest tree," said coal. "I was a *fern* tree. Nowadays, you have something hugging the ground you call a fern, but who knows where they came from? I was a real tree with a tall and enormous trunk, and a spacious crown. Such trees filled the entire forest and, as for people, well, there just weren't any people then."

"That's ridiculous," interrupted firewood, who got told to shut up by peat and coke.

"Carry on coal," said coke.

"Not only were there no people, neither were there any birds, deer, bears or other animals you mentioned. Nowadays, there are only these small things like insects since everything on the earth is reduced in size. But then, there were enormous lizard-like animals standing on two legs, some as tall as trees that crawled all over the rocks. Some of similar sizes swarmed in the lakes, and still others flew. If you can imagine those, then you have a vague idea of the animals I lived amongst in my youth. Well, I can remember it, anyway."

"On the way over here, I saw a little tiny animal sunning itself on a rock. The train conductor called it a lizard. If you have seen it and can imagine it about a thousand times as large with a scary jaw full of pointed teeth, then you have a vague idea of the animals I lived amongst in my youth."

"You've got to call that quite a story," said peat respectfully.

"That's how it was for me; we stood like that for miles around. But, it's also true..." coal went silent and sighed.

"Go on," said coke.

"Well," said coal, "you don't even know what the land was like in those days, and I can't make it real for you. It differed totally from today, but I need to pass over that. I couldn't help laughing before when peat told us about the lake it fell into. Good heavens, that was just a puddle, but we must move on."

"There I was, standing tall hundreds of thousands of years ago when an earthquake struck—a real one. It wasn't like a storm that broke off a few miserable branches; the whole earth trembled, and the ground split open, rocks broke into pieces, and everything slid down into the abyss and got crushed. Fires sprung from the earth, and then the ocean came up, washing over everything."

"Terrible," said peat.

"Indeed," said coke.

"So, I lay there," said coal, "hidden, and buried in the sand and clay, and goodness knows what else and I don't have the slightest idea of what happened up here in the world for the hundreds of thousands of years that went by before I saw daylight again. I can only observe from everything I now see. Now that's how big a step backwards it was since my time."

"Thanks, we're aware of that," said firewood. "That's the way all old timers talk. I remember the day when two aging ladies were sitting in the shade I provided and gossiped about how lovely girls were when they were in their prime."

Coal became quiet.

"Is that all?" asked firewood when coal became quiet.

"No, there is more" said coal. "I was just thinking how strange it is for me to hear all this talk about people, old ladies, and girls which I know nothing about even though I'm hundreds of times older than the oldest of you."

"But what happened... you know... down in the ground?" asked peat.

"Well, there I was, lying by myself, and you cannot understand how much pressure I had to bear over me from everything above. Fire was burning inside me, not like a flickering flame that bites the air when an insignificant pile of firewood burns, but rather it raged like a smoldering inferno which completely transformed me. Everything that was hardy and strong in me took on such a perfectly unruly, impossible presence you simply cannot understand it, but it's called 'gas'."

"Oh yuk! Yes... it's the gas," said coke, which began to cry uncontrollably.

"I told you that my story would get on your nerves horribly," said coal.

"Just keep gooo...ing," said coke, whimpering with every word.

"I think the earth had collapsed and raised itself up again, and oceans had washed over it and rushed away many, many times in the many hundreds of thousands of years I was lying there," said coal. "I remember nothing about that. But one day, I met my first humans, these people you always talk about; they drilled down into me, and I saw them closely. They dug great passageways down into the mountain where I was lying, long deep ones, the one longer and deeper than the other that went this way and that. It's called a ***mine shaft***."

"They shattered me and others away from the layers of rock we were embedded in and hauled us up to the surface in baskets. We killed a lot of these people while they were working because just as soon as we hit the air, we released the gas inside us and suffocated them. If the least little fire came near us, our gas exploded with an incredible ferociousness, breaking us up into bits and pieces, and killing everyone in the passageways."

"Ugh! The gas!" sobbed coke rocking back and forth, unable to contain its pain.

"I'm almost done," said coal. "The entire world knows the rest of my story. I flourished on the earth as the proudest tree in the forest before there were people, and I remained like that totally without their help. But when they finally discovered me, I was a bigger help to them than anything they had found previously. I'm the world's most superior form of fuel. I drive all the world's factories, railroads, steamships—like the one I came here on—everything. I have more heat in me than anyone else. And from me comes... the gas."

"Oh, the gas - the gas!" It was coke groaning again.

"That's my story," said coal. "I guess that beats all of yours."

"It does," said peat.

"It seems like it's also the last story we'll hear," said firewood. "Coke doesn't look like it can hold up to tell us its story."

"Well now I can," said coke. "Let me collect myself, and I'll be right there."

So, coke pulled itself together and told this story.

Chapter 5 — Coke's Story

❝I was once the proudest tree in the forest…"
You can't imagine how the woodshed reacted when coke began its story with those words. Firewood broke out laughing, and coal laughed so hard that the place reeked of gas. Peat just rolled over into a corner and giggled, and they all made such a noise that the rat came charging in under the door.

"I think there's someone here," he said and sniffed around but left after not finding anything.

"My dear coke," said coal when they had recovered somewhat. "I suppose your nerves are plainly frayed to a high degree. Or did you have a little attack of making yourself more important than you really are?"

"What a tree you must have been!" said firewood. "If only I had seen you in all your glory and magnificence."

"Pardon me," said peat. "I also laughed when the others did, even if it was a bit rude of me. But shouldn't we let coke finish up with its story?"

"Tell us more,' said firewood. "It's bound to be a rip-roaring story."

"On the contrary," said coke. "My story is extremely sad, and not because I think your stories are especially funny. But in my case, they treated me worse yet, even though I am a blood brother to coal."

"Now, that's a bit much, my friend," said coal.

"It's true," said coke.

"Ha, Ha!" laughed firewood. "I swear you two amazingly resemble each other when one looks really closely at you."

"I protest!" said coal. "Look at me and look at coke… porous and pitiful and light as a feather! Anybody can see that coke is a miserable excuse, not worth two cents, and now look at me. I'm hard, I'm heavy, and I shine. And realize, also, that I'm a first cousin to a diamond."

"That's true of me, too," said coke, "and it's not very nice of you to disown me. If they treated you as I was, you wouldn't look better yourself."

"Let's hear your story," said firewood.

"You shouldn't believe a word," said coal.

*   *   *

"I'm from England, too, just like coal," said coke. "I grew up in the same forest and began like coal as the same fern tree hundreds of thousands of years ago. My story is exactly like coal's is, until ..."

Coke became silent, too moved to say anything.

"Well?" said firewood.

"Give coke a chance to regain its composure," said peat.

But coke broke into a sobbing so shattering that it was about to crumble into pieces.... "right until they burned the gas out of me," coke said finally.

"Dear me," said coal. "Is that possible?"

"It's true, and I'm not making it up", said coke. "We were dug out of the coal mine, hoisted up in the same baskets, and arrived here on land from England in the same ship. But at that point, we went different ways. They brought me to the gasworks where they locked me into a huge bin and heated me until all the gas had escaped. They then sold me cheaply to poor folks with small houses. They may well put you in the grand fireplaces in the huge rooms of the big houses, but I'm used in the tiny rooms where the servants live!"

Coke cried and cried, and the others showed respect for coke's loss because now they understood.

"It's all strange," said firewood thoughtfully.

"I can't figure it out," blubbered coke.

"If I had fallen into the swamp, I might have become a pile of peat," said firewood.

"And if they had cut me down hundreds of thousands of years ago, I could have been firewood," said coal.

"If I had lain for ninety-nine thousand years in the swamp, I'd surely have ended up like coal," said peat.

"And if they hadn't taken all the gas out of me…" said coke. But it couldn't say any more.

For a moment it was silent in the woodshed. Everyone was thinking of their own story until peat finally said:

"Now I've got it."

"What have you got?" asked firewood.

"Well, knock me over," said peat, "but I've just realized that we're all cousins, four chips off the old block."

The Old Willow Tree

Chapter 1

There are many kinds of willow trees that don't look at all alike. Who could possibly guess that they're all in the same family? There are some that are so small and miserable looking that they creep along the ground. Those are found in the moors, or high up in the mountains, or in the cold polar regions. In the winter, they are completely hidden, covered by snow, and in the summer, they can just get their tops above the heather.

Like the willows, some people cower in their poverty, but no one should be ashamed of being poor. The dwarf willows certainly aren't' like that, but they know that the ground they are growing in is so greatly impoverished that they won't be developing into respectable trees. They understand that they'll never reach upward and tower into the sky like their distinguished cousins, the poplars.

The poplars are the most distinguished of all the trees in the willow family, of course, and anyone can see with eyes half-closed that the poplars know this. Just look at how they keep themselves so erect, and it becomes clear. The beech, the oak, the birch and whatever all the other trees are called, merely extend a courteous limb out on one side and stick another welcome limb out on the other side.

"How about a bit of sunshine?" the respectful limb says up in the air.

"A bit of shade, maybe?" the twigs say near the ground.

But among the poplars, you'll hear a different tune:

"All you limbs, straighten up and stay close to the trunk. There's nothing worth seeing down below, so look up now, stretch, and reach for the sky!"

And all the poplar branches proudly burst, shooting upwards into the air, tall and proud. It's an effort, but it's a grand feeling and it pays off. Has anyone ever seen a lovelier tree than a genuine, erect poplar? Stiff like a tin soldier, and as tall as a church steeple! Standing in long rows on both sides of a road, they gain your total admiration as you wander among them, and you are hardly surprised when they lead you right up to a beautiful manor house.

So, the dwarf willow and the poplar are perhaps the two extremes of this large family. One of them is just plain-looking, and the other is unquestionably grandiose, but there are many other willow types. Some have leaves that are silvery on one side, and some whose leaves tremble so wistfully in the warm summer breezes that poets write verses about them.

Some have limbs hanging so mournfully down toward the ground that people plant them near gravesites, and some whose branches are so tough and flexible that people use them for weaving baskets. Some you can use to whittle into a great flute if you have the talent for it, but there's a lot that have nothing special about them. The willow tree in this story is one of those, but it had an inevitable fate, and that's what I'll tell you about.

Chapter 2

Our tale begins when one of the proud poplars standing in the driveway leading up to the manor house was blown over in an awful storm. With the roots upended, the trunk was cut up, and the stump was dug out, but the scene looked ugly with the large hole in the long lineup of trees. As soon as spring arrived, the groundskeeper came by with a **tree cutting** and stuck it down into the hole where the old poplar had stood. He stamped the ground well around it and nodded at the tree cutting.

"Be quick now, and reach for the sky," he said. "I know it's in your sap, and all you need to do is look down the carriageway to see some great examples to imitate."

The groundskeeper believed that it was a poplar tree he had planted, but actually, it was only a perfectly ordinary willow branch cutting he had chosen by mistake. As time went on and the cutting grew, he realized what a mistake he had made.

"What a monstrosity," said the groundskeeper. "We need to get that one out again"

"Let it stay there since it's growing fine," interrupted the Master of the estate who was in a tolerant mood and just expressing how he felt that day.

"Should we tolerate it?" asked the poplars down the row.

The proud poplars whispered about this among themselves for a long time, but since no one knew how to be rid of the growing tree cutting, they ended up accepting it. After all, it did belong to the family even if it wasn't from one of the most respectable species.

"Now, listen: You must do your very best to straighten up as much as possible," said the nearest poplar. "You've come into some very dignified company, you understand. With your branches pointing downwards and sideways instead of up to the sky, you'd have fit better by a village pond than in the driveway of the master's estate. But now that the scandal of your even being here is decided, we'll just try covering for you. We'll straighten ourselves up and get a trifle thinner and just hope that the distinguished people driving by won't pay any attention to you."

"I'll do my best to fit in," said the humbled willow tree.

On a little hill situated in a field close by, an oak tree was standing, and next to his trunk a lovely wild rosebush was also growing. They had both heard what the promenade poplars were talking about, and the oak began to scoff at them. Then he spoke to the willow tree.

"How can you stand to be sitting out there on the promenade. Did you plan on running up and down like those silly soldier trees? It was both mean and dumb of your parent tree to put you there. You ought to be hidden among other trees in a forest, since you're not a pretty specimen. You have no pride in yourself like I do, which is why I can stand alone."

"My descendent parent didn't put me here at all," replied the willow tree.

"Oh, for pity sake," said the oak. "Your descendent parent didn't plant you there at all? I suppose the others weren't placed there either. You've all just dropped from the sky."

"If you had opened your eyes, you would have seen that the groundskeeper put me here," said the willow tree. "I'm from a tree cutting."

And far down on the carriageway, the poplars whispered to each other: "But we were of the right cuttings, and he never used one of us."

We are the right cuttings, the right cutting, the right cuttings!" it echoed down the carriageway.

*   *   *

It was a magnificent carriageway. A true promenade for the master's estate.

"You handled that oak well," said the poplar closest to the willow tree. "Just keep doing what you've begun, and we'll forgive you that you're not nearly so distinguished as we are."

"I'll do my best," replied the willow tree.

The oak tree didn't respond. It only knew about acorns and nothing about cuttings and so it didn't want to say something that might sound stupid. But toward evening the oak whispered to the wild rose: "What kind of nonsense was that about 'cuttings'?"

"It's not really nonsense," replied the wild rosebush. "It's just like the willow tree said. For myself, I almost certainly grew from a seed just like you did, and I never did see the groundskeeper plant the willow tree because on that day I was so busy with my own buds. But I do have some fine cousins up at the estate's garden. They also grew from cuttings, and their fragrance is so sweet, their colors so striking, and their blossoms with so many petals, you'd never believe it. But neither do they produce any seeds, strangely."

"Can you believe it?" said the oak.

"Yes, I'd rather be the wild rose I am," said the rosebush.

Chapter 3

The seasons and many years passed, and the rains came, along with snow, sunshine, storms, good days and bad ones. Birds flew away and returned. Flowers blossomed out and withered; trees leafed out before dropping them at the right time in the fall.

The willow cutting flourished as is characteristic of the family it belongs to. It was now a fully-grown tree with a thick trunk and many large limbs in its crown. But it could not be denied; it certainly was no poplar—the complete opposite in appearance, in fact—and the willows' family members down the carriageway line were very annoyed with it.

"Isn't there some way you could thin down a bit and put some more height on you?" asked the nearest poplar. "You really should never have been here in the first place, but since you came into the row by an unfortunate accident, I do wish that you would stretch a bit higher up into the air."

"I'll do my best," said the willow tree.

"I'm afraid that your best will not be good enough," said the poplar. "You don't have any hold on your limbs to keep them in the air; they just hang out loosely on all sides. It's almost as bad as if you were an ordinary beech or birch or oak tree, or whatever else those common trees are called."

"Did you call me common, you windbag?" said the oak.

The poplar didn't give a hoot what the oak said but continued to scold the willow tree.

"You should try to imitate our master's wife," said the poplar. "In the beginning, she was just an ordinary kitchen girl. She scrubbed the pots and pans, started the fire, and stirred the gruel. I've seen her many times walking in the carriageway with a bucket in her hand, with her arms and head uncovered, and her dress tucked up."

"We saw it too...we saw it too...we saw it too," echoed far down the row of poplars.

"Then the master fell in love with her, and made her his wife," said the poplar. "Now she walks around in silks with a train, and an ostrich feather on her head, gold shoes on her feet, and long gloves from Paris. She looks down on everything from above like yesterday when she drove down here in her fine coach drawn by four chestnut-colored horses."

"We saw her too...we saw her too...we saw her too," echoed far down the row of poplars.

"She came into the carriageway, you understand," said the poplar. "She has learned to hold her head up high; she whispers gently, never too loud. I think you could learn from her example. You come from the right family, even if you're not a genuine poplar, and so it must be easier for you than for her."

"I'll do my best," said the willow tree.

But nothing changed. Branches continued growing out from the sides, and the entire tree was not half as tall as the lowest of the poplars. Incidentally, it was really a very cozy and lovely tree, but that is beside the point in a world of distinguished poplar company.

The poplars became more and more annoyed for every day that passed. They stood erect and straight, providing no more shade than their trunks allowed, whereas under the willow tree, there was a really expansive shaded area.

"It's a disgrace to the whole carriageway," said the nearest poplar.

"The whole carriageway, the whole carriageway, the whole carriageway," echoed down the row of poplars.

✳   ✳   ✳

One really warm summer's day, as the master was walking around, he took off his hat, wiped the sweat from his brow, and sought the shade of the willow tree.

"Thanks so much for your shade, you fine willow tree," he said. "Those damned poplars stand there so straight and don't provide more shade than the back of my hand. I think I'll chop them all down and plant willow trees instead," which was just how he was feeling that day.

"Did you hear how the master praised me," said the willow tree after the master had left.

"Heavens!" said the nearest poplar. "Did we hear it? It's a complete scandal! He talked just like he was a common farmer. That must come from his marrying that dreadful kitchen girl. It will always be true: stick to your own class."

"Stick to your own class...your own class...your own class..." echoed down the carriageway.

The oak tree on the little hill out in the field shook its twisted limbs in laughter while the wild rose, whose growing hips were already beginning to redden, nodded to the willow tree.

"Each to its own," said the wild rose. "We have ours, and the fine folks have theirs. I wouldn't change for anyone."

"You need to know your place and be satisfied," said the willow tree sighing.

Chapter 4

After the warm days, came drizzles, hard rains, and strong winds. The roads were treacherous to walk on due to mud and slush. Only in the driveway did it immediately become dry again regardless of how much it rained, and this was due to how little shade the poplars provided, allowing the sunshine to come through just as soon as the rain stopped. And the poplars didn't serve as a windbreak either, so the puddles were quickly dried up.

The master came driving by with his mistress, and when the coach came to the spot where the willow tree was standing, the ground was still wet, and the mud splashed up onto her new silk dress.

"Ugh!" she said.

"That's disgusting," said the master.

The groundskeeper who was sitting on a seat next to the coach driver pointed to the willow tree.

"That's the culprit there," he said. "It's the willow, planted by mistake, and it's gotten so large it provides a windbreak, and good shade from the sun. There's always a puddle under it long after the rest of the carriageway is dry."

"That's just intolerable," said the master. "Look how it sits there just destroying the view of my tall distinguished poplars all in a row. Groundskeeper, be sure to take it down tomorrow," he said because that was just how he was feeling that day. "I want the whole crown off. Do you hear me?"

The next day they came and topped the willow tree, so it was only as tall as a man. Only the thick, naked trunk remained. There wasn't a single leaf left except for a little branch nearly touching the ground that had five leaves on it.

Actually, that branch shouldn't have been there in the first place, but the groundskeeper had missed it. The entire remainder of the beautiful crown of the tree was now lying in a ditch, all the boughs chopped into small pieces with an axe.

"Will you use them for cuttings?" asked the now decapitated willow tree downheartedly.

"They'll be used as firewood," replied the groundskeeper, chopping away to the last log.

"In that case, I'd rather die immediately," said the willow tree.

"Presently, you can stay here for the winter," said the forester. "When the heavy snow piles up everywhere, you'll serve as a good indicator of where the carriageway ditch lies. What happens afterwards is for the master to decide."

"That's a lovely ending to *The Willow Cutting's Finale*," barked the oak tree.

"The poor willow tree," said the wild rosebush.

"Thanks for your concern," said the willow tree. "I'm still a bit puzzled. It's not just having lost my entire crown, but rather it is not knowing what's going to happen to me next."

"It's just an awful scandal," said the nearest poplar. "A scandal in the family without precedent. If only they would just come and take you completely away, so you wouldn't stand there and disgrace us with your disgusting, wretched trunk."

"A family scandal...scandal...scandal," echoed down the driveway.

"I don't feel awful in the least, strangely enough," said the willow tree. "I don't even know if I've done anything to be ashamed of. I was put here and did my best to fill up the space. The master praised me one day and cut me down the next. You've got to take life as it comes. I'll never develop into some kind of a poplar, but I'm still a respectable member of the family, which has other characteristics than mere pride. Let's now look to the years ahead to see what happens to me."

"That's talking like a human," said the wild rosebush.

The oak tree didn't say a word. The poplars whistled with pride but spoke no more about the family scandal.

Chapter 5

The master and his mistress traveled to Italy and remained down there for a couple of years. That meant the decapitated willow tree was allowed to grow in peace among the poplars again. Since the master and mistress were absent, there was no one around to worry about the favorable appearance of the carriageway.

Through the winter, missing its crown, the willow tree stood silent and disheartened. It's totally understandable that you wouldn't feel much like talking if the better part of you were missing. But well into March, the willow tree suddenly began to cry out in misery.

"Oh, my head! my head!" it screamed.

"I've never in all my days heard such a fuss," said the oak tree. "If it's not talking about its crown, then it's plain for anyone to see that its been topped off, so there's nothing left but a miserable stump."

"It's easy for you to talk," said the willow tree. "You should be in my place. My entire crown is gone, including all the largest boughs and the little branches where my new buds were waiting for next year, each in its own leaf axil. But I've still got all of my roots... all those that I put out when I had a large household to take care of. The ground is thawing, the sun is beginning to shine, and the roots are sucking and drawing up nutrients but without all my branches, they have nowhere to go. Oh, I think, I'm exploding, I'm going to die!"

"The poor willow tree," said the rosebush.

But up on the other side of the little hill, there was an elder bush that no one talked to and which usually never wanted to say anything.

"You'll see, it'll be fine from Wednesday until Saturday," it finally said. "But now listen to what a poor, yet honest, elder bush has to say. In the end, it's going to work out one way or the other for you."

"You've sure had some unusual experiences," said the oak tree.

"Yes, indeed," said the elder bush. "They've chopped me down; they've clipped me, topped me, and dismembered me in every possible way. But every time they went at me from one end, I shot out at the other. That's the way the willow tree will do it too. It's also a member of a stubborn family."

"Did you all hear that?" said the nearest poplar tree. "The elder bush is comparing his family with ours! Let's just pretend we never heard it... we'll just straighten up and whistle as usual."

"We'll just straighten up and whistle...whistle... whistle ...," echoed far down the carriageway.

"What are those funny little things up at the top of the willow tree?" inquired the oak tree. "Just look at them, they're swelling way up at the top. They're probably some kind of junk growth and they had better not infect us."

"Heavens, no, those are my buds," said the willow tree. "I don't understand it, but I sure can feel it. They are real, living buds, and I'm going to green up again. I'm going to get a new crown!"

The very busiest time of the year arrived, with plenty to do for all, and so no one had time to think about the poor willow tree. The proud poplars and the poor elder bush flushed out with new leaves. The grass greened up on the edge of the ditches, the grain was growing in the fields, and the wild rose bush sent out its fine leaves so that the flowers would look their best look when they came out in June. The violets and anemones bloomed and died; daisies, pansies, dandelions, wild chervil, and parsley... really, it was such spectacle, such a happy scene everywhere. The birds sang as they had never sung before, the frogs croaked in the pond, and the grass snake was lying on the stone wall sunning its black body.

The only creature not taking part in this joyful awakening was the oak tree. It was by nature suspicious of change and would not

under any circumstances bud out in leaf before it saw that all the others were greened up first. It stood there, peeking from one side to the next, and was the first to discover what had happened to the willow tree.

"Look! the surprised oak screamed.

They all looked over and saw that the willow tree was standing with a whole bunch of lovely, long, curving green stems shooting straight up in the air, swaying with gorgeous leaves. All the stems were sitting so stately in a wreath around the chopped off trunk, that no poplar needed to be ashamed of it.

"I told you so," said the elder bush standing with a bunch of dark green leaves.

"I have a crown again," said the willow tree, "and even if it's not nearly as lovely as the old one... but a crown it is, which nobody will be able to deny."

"Of course," said the wild rose. "It's only natural. Oh, didn't you know it's very easy to live happily without a crown. I don't have one, I've never had one, and I've never lacked respect and standing for it."

"If you want my honest opinion, a crown is a real nuisance," said the elder bush. "I had one once, but I'm a lot more satisfied since they took it from me, and I can now send out my branches just as I like."

"That's not how I feel," said the willow tree. "I'm a tree, and a tree needs a crown. If I had not been blessed with a crown, I would surely have died of sorrow and shame."

"There are still poplar traits in it," said the nearest poplar.

The other poplars whistled approvingly... "poplar traits, poplar traits, poplar traits", all down the carriageway.

"Let's see what happens now," said the oak.

Chapter 6

Summer arrived, and the sun shone so much on every living thing that they pleaded for rain. Then it rained so much that everyone shouted to heaven for it to stop and let the sun shine again.

The willow tree was now quite content. By nature, it is easily satisfied, and it was so happy over its new crown that it realized it could get along with whatever came its way. Up at the top, right in the circle of the green branches, there was a hole in the trunk that had appeared when the groundkeeper had lopped off the crown. The hole wasn't that small though, and after a rain, it was full of water which lasted a good while even after the ground dried out again.

One day a blackbird came flying in and landed at the hole up in the tree. "Will you permit me to have a drop of water, old willow tree?" said the blackbird.

"My pleasure," said the willow tree. "By the way, I'm not so old, so you must be making fun of me."

"Oh yes," said the blackbird. "You've been clipped, and we all know it. Such a sight you are now."

"Well then, can you also dry your feet off," said the willow tree curtly. "You mustn't muddy the water for anyone else who might come to drink. You never know in this drought."

The blackbird wiped his feet against a splinter of wood close by the hole, and when he flew off, the splinter of wood loosened leaving a little mound of dirt behind. The next day, a swallow came by, and then a lark and eventually many other birds flew in because it soon became generally known that, if necessary, you could always get a drop of water in the carriageway where the sawed-off willow tree was standing. And everyone who visited left a little bit of this and a little bit of that behind, and so one bright day in the fall there was so such accumulating debris that the dirt mound collapsed filling up the hole which provided the water.

"You've been keeping a regular public drinking place there," said the oak.

"Why shouldn't I be a friend to my fellow creatures?" replied the willow tree.

*   *   *

Fall came and the withered leaves of the willow tree blew away, settling down finally where they laid and rotted. A dragonfly had managed to die in late summer up in the place where the hole was, and one of the dandelion's fluffy seeds had descended into the same place right by its side. Winter came, and the snow fell on the little spot where it remained just the right amount of time, exactly as it does down on the ground.

"It feels just exactly as if I have a whole piece of the world in my new crown," said the willow tree.

"It's not healthy to have too much in your crown," added the oak.

"I once had a large, marvelous crown," said the willow tree sadly. "But now I'm content with less. You have to take life as it comes."

"That's right," said the wild rosebush.

"It'll all work out," said the elder bush. "I've said that before."

"Hardy fellow," said the nearest poplar.

"Hardy fellow... hardy fellow... hardy fellow," echoed all down the carriageway.

Chapter 7

Winter left, and spring arrived and up at the top of the willow tree, a little green shoot was peeking out in the middle of the hole.

"Goodness, who are you?" asked the willow tree.

"I'm just a little dandelion," said the green shoot. "I was sitting at the top of my parent, together with all my numerous siblings. We each had a little parachute on. "Fly away now, little ones," came the instructions. "The further away you fly, the better. I'm done nurturing you, but I won't deny that I'm a bit worried about all of you; the world is so big. But I can't do it over again, and I hope that you'll all find a little spot where a decent dandelion can thrive."

"Yes, that's just what a little flower parent would say to her young," said the wild rosebush.

"What happened after that?" asked the willow tree.

"A gust of wind then came along," said the young dandelion. "We all flew up into the air, carried by our parachutes. I have no idea where all the others went, but I do remember it began to rain on me, and so I was thrown down here. I thought, of course, that as soon as I dried out, I could fly further, but nothing came of that because my parachute had been torn to bits. So, I had to stay where I was, but amazingly, I realized that I was lying on firm ground. Eventually even more ground piled up on the same spot I was hiding in all winter, and now I'm a green shoot. Now, you have the whole story."

"What a story, like a fairy tale come true," said the wild rosebush.

"That may be so," said the dandelion. "But what's going to happen to me in the future? Honestly, I'd really like to be down on the ground again."

"I'll do everything for you in my power," said the willow tree. "I've also experienced tough times, but it's a great honor and joy to have you growing in my poor crown."

"Thanks so much for your kind friendship," said the dandelion. "Indeed, there's not so much of that in the world, so when it's offered, shouldn't one appreciate it? But when all is said and done, it's your ability that counts, and that's where I think it's going to be hard for me."

"I know just what you're thinking," said the willow tree sadly. "I can't provide you any shade since the groundskeeper topped off my beautiful crown. My long branches up there are satisfactory, those that are even worth mentioning, and I certainly wouldn't do without them, but they cannot provide shade. I'll never get another real crown, of course. Are you afraid that the sun will shine down too hard on you?"

"Oh, on the contrary," said the dandelion. "The more sunshine I get in my golden face, the happier I am. No, you, it's your soil I'm worried about."

"It's also the most important element," said the oak. "But that's the willow tree's business. If it wants to make a proper niche for flowers in its head, then it will naturally have to go about getting some soil."

"Yes, but isn't there some soil here, my dear dandelion?" asked the willow tree.

"It's not that, soil is there," said the dandelion, "and it's good quality too, but I'm just worried that there isn't enough of it. I'm telling you I have an awfully long root—it can be quite surprising, I assure you. When I'm all grown up, it goes six inches down into the dirt."

"Well now," said the oak. "Imagine such a skimpy fellow talking about roots."

The willow tree paused a second, saying nothing but thinking a lot. The wild rosebush consoled the dandelion, saying nice things about the willow tree, and the elder bush said that it would all work out. However, the oak grumbled and asked whether you could expect anything decent, after all, from a tree lacking a crown.

"Now listen here," said the willow tree who had not been listening to what the others were saying. "I'm going to tell you something, my dear dandelion, that I don't normally like to mention. Do you know that I was abused and lost my crown?"

"I heard you say that before," said the dandelion. "I can also see that compared to the other trees in the carriageway, you seem to be somewhat down in the dumps."

"Don't talk about the poplars," said the willow tree unhappily. "They are my relatives, but they've never forgiven that I was planted here by mistake as a tree cutting. Look at them and then look at me, and you'll be able to judge for yourself how such a messed-up creature like me appears as a disgrace to a row of distinguished poplars."

"It still knows its place," said the nearest poplar. And all the other poplar trees down the carriageway echoed their agreement.

"You're thinking too much about it," said the elder bush. "The more you worry about it, the worse it becomes. I'd have gone to my grave long ago if I kept rehashing and crying over all the suffering I've had."

"Yes, well it's not that important," said the willow tree. "Each of us makes the best of it, and I do it in my own way. I'm not intending to surrender at all, but I also know that I'm deformed and will never be anything else. I considered originally that my long, new branches up there could become another crown, but it was stupid of me. They'll grow, stiffen, and green up, but I'll never experience more than that. I feel already that I'm beginning to rot away.

"What's that you're saying?" said the wild rosebush.

"Are you rotting?" asked the oak tree.

"That would surely be the worst thing," said the elder bush.

"Bah! the willow tree is sharing its deepest secrets with the peasantry," said the nearest poplar haughtily. "Let's stiffen up, stand erect, and keep each other informed, as we reach for the sky, my carriageway brothers." And all the poplars whispered their usual chorus of agreement.

"Indeed, I'm rotting," said the willow tree, ignoring the snobbish poplars. "I'm rotting at the top. How could it be otherwise? There's a regular lake up in my hole in the summer, there's snow in the winter, and it's now full of damp soil. I can clearly feel that the hole is getting larger and larger, and going deeper and deeper into me. My wood is crumbling, even if my shell is still good enough. I'm happy as long as it lasts. Then the sap from my roots will still be able to rise up to my dear, long branches. Gosh... I even think that the birds will come to visit me as they usually do, bringing constantly more dirt with them, and making the hole deeper yet. They also deposit their droppings and plenty of withered leaves fall too on my poor, mutilated top. I'm also sure that I have an earthworm busy up there, but I have no idea how it came, unless a bird dropped it from its beak. Worms drag the leaves under the ground, eat them and convert them to humus and so I say as the elder bush does: 'it all works out', but it'll mean the end for me."

"So, are you actually going to become a hollow tree?" inquired the oak.

"Yes, I will," said the willow tree. "There's nothing I can do about that. It's not a subject you normally talk about, but the dandelion was really quite worried about it. No one is going to accuse me of boarding a harmless flower and letting it pine away for fear of dying."

"Has anyone ever heard a tree talk like that," said the oak.

"No indeed, I also have to agree with you," said the wild rosebush.

"I don't think the willow tree will last much longer," said the elder bush.

"Thanks a lot, old willow tree, my friend," said the dandelion. "Now I can grow up with confidence. I have actually only this year left to think about it. When I've broadcast my seeds with their small parachutes, then I've done all that is required of me. It would make me very happy if one of them will stay here and continue to grow inside you."

"Thanks a lot," said the willow tree, feeling better to be consoled by the rosebush and the elder bush. It thanked the dandelion, but as for its closest neighbors when it said to them: 'We're in the same family,' the nearest poplar replied: "Disgusting!"

"Disgusting...disgusting...disgusting!" echoed down the long carriageway.

Chapter 8

Evening came, then nightfall, and almost everyone was asleep. The wind had calmed down so there wasn't the slightest rustle in the poplars. The oak tree on the little hill in the field looked around and then called to the willow tree.

"Psst... psst, willow tree. Are you sleeping?"

"I can't sleep," said the willow tree. "My hole is rumbling, grumbling, oozing, and seething, and I'm sure that it's sinking deeper and deeper inside me. It makes me feel so melancholy."

"It can't be good becoming a hollow tree," said the oak.

"Indeed," said the willow tree sadly. "But there's nothing I can do about it; I can't avoid my fate."

"Now listen here, willow tree," said the oak tree. "Basically, I don't like you."

"I didn't know that I had done anything to you to deserve that," said the willow tree.

"Maybe so," replied the oak, "but I thought you were so vain even when you first appeared as a cutting. Now it doesn't matter that I feel so terribly sorry for you ever since I heard that you were in the process of becoming a hollowed-out tree, because you don't seem to want to do anything about it, and that's terribly unfortunate."

"I sure don't know how I'm supposed to react to prevent it," said the willow tree.

"I don't know either," said the oak tree, "but can't you at least try something. See if you can't get the birds visiting you to scrape out all the dirt accumulating in the hole in your crown before it gets too deep."

"But I couldn't do anything to hurt the dandelion," said the willow tree. "There isn't any real danger yet, I don't think. My branches are still green and thriving, and my roots are sucking up nutrients well enough. As you know, everything is fine as long as my roots are functioning well."

"Just watch out," said the oak tree. "You don't know what's involved, but I do. I'll tell you this: I have an old, hollowed-out relative."

"Do you?" said the willow tree. "Well, there are always some skeletons in every family's closet. You have yours, and the poplars have me."

"You have no idea what kind of a life it leads," said the oak tree. "It's terribly old, and terribly hollowed-out. Yes, in a sense it resembles you, but it's in horribly worse shape than you are.

There's not much left; there's only a thin shell of itself with a miserable branch at the top. Almost all of its roots are also dead, and it's constantly full of owls, bats, and other vermin. It leads a miserable life."

"It makes me sad to hear that," said the willow tree.

"I'm telling you: be cautious!" said the oak tree.

Chapter 9

The years came and went, and disregarding the oak's suggestion, the willow tree kept rotting even more, its hole filling up with more dirt and accepting more visitors. One spring, a little green shoot appeared that the willow tree welcomed thinking it was a new dandelion.

"Well now," said the green shoot, "what do you think about me?"

"I have the very best opinion of you," said the willow tree. "But you're still so small. Tell me, what is your name?"

"I'm a strawberry plant," said the green shoot. "And one of the finest there is. I believe that I'm the equal of those growing in the master's garden. Just wait until I bear fruit, and then you'll all see what I mean."

"My goodness," said the willow tree. "If only I could figure out where you've come from."

Another green shoot appeared, which announced itself as the beginning of a black currant bush. A third one came along which would grow to be a lovely rowan berry bush and so it went on. The hollow got bigger and bigger and every summer, a couple of dandelions always showed their pretty faces. The bees came buzzing around, sucking up the nectar and flying home with it to put in their hives. Butterflies flitted from flower to flower, sucking up a little nectar here and there, and eating it at once. Their lives were short, so there was nothing to save it for.

"It's just wonderful," said the willow tree. "If only I knew where all this happiness springs from."

"You shouldn't ask, but just enjoy it as it comes," said the elder bush.

"You're having a beautiful old age," said the wild rosebush.

"You're getting hollower and hollower," said the oak. "Remember what I told you about my poor old relative."

"The willow is getting forgetful," said the nearest poplar.

"Getting forgetful... getting forgetful... getting forgetful," echoed down the long carriageway.

The blackbird who was the first to visit the willow tree, had done so repeatedly for many years. One day it arrived in a great tizzy, begging its friend to hide in its straggly crown. A terrible boy had been shooting at it all morning with a small rifle when it was off-season for bird hunting.

"I'm protected this time of the year*," said the blackbird, "no one here is supposed to hunt me but what does a rotten kid care about that? And if it comes to ending life, why can't it happen by being caught in a proper snare?"

"I think it would be better to be shot," said the willow tree. "Then it's all over in a second.

"I don't think so," said the blackbird. "As long as there is life, there is hope. You're always hung up in the trap, squirming around, but still believing that you can get out."

"Oh yes, I see," said the willow tree thoughtfully. "When I weigh the pros and cons, it's about the same for me. I'm in a trap too, and I know that death is there, but I continue living anyway.

Well... I've had a blessed old age as the wild rosebush said. If only I knew where all those dear creatures that are growing on top of me came from."

"I can certainly tell you about that," said the blackbird. "You can rest assured that most of them have come from me."

The blackbird told how keen it was for red berries of one or another kind. It especially liked to take refuge in the master's garden which was loaded with the tastiest offerings. When later it was sitting in the willow tree digesting its food, it usually left some seeds thing in its droppings.

"Is that it?" said the willow tree. "Well, yes, of course that's how it happens," agreed the willow tree. "So, I really owe all my happiness of providing life to others—to you?

"Apparently," said the blackbird whistling conceitedly. "Thank heaven we all have our missions in life, but... let me see now; I think I see a lovely ripe strawberry on you."

He pecked and ate the strawberry, saying 'Aah', 'Ooh' and 'Yum' with each nibble because it had such a delicious flavor.

"It's exactly like those growing in the master's own garden beds," he said. "But I almost think it has a more delicious flavor from growing up here on you, old willow tree."

"Dear blackbird," said the strawberry plant. "You come frequently to the master's garden. Won't you do me the favor of telling the master that I'm growing up here?"

"I most certainly will not," said the blackbird. "First of all, it would never occur to me to tell anyone a thing about where a good berry is found. Secondly, I'm gradually getting so heavy and fat that I need to be a bit careful. Otherwise it might occur to the master that strawberries taste twice as good on top of roast bird."

"That's really too bad," said the strawberry bush. "I know that the master has said that he won't eat any strawberries except those from our variety, and there are so few of us. I've also heard a bird sing that the master has returned from Italy, and I'm sure that if he knew that I was growing up here, he'd come crawling up here himself to pick my berries."

"Heavens, save and protect me!" responded the willow tree. "Am I really to have the master himself crawling around in my crown? I can't imagine I'd be so honored."

"And so, you really shouldn't," said the oak, "because you're getting hollower and hollower by the day. Your long branches aren't even as green this year, and. you're beginning to resemble my poor relative more and more. You're approaching the end of your life, willow tree."

"You may be right," said the willow tree wistfully. "No one escapes his fate. I feel it myself; my trunk is getting thinner and thinner, and now there are holes in it at two places down below."

"Away with her," said the nearest poplar. "She's a mess and shames the entire family."

"Away... away... away," echoed down the long carriageway. "She's a mess and shames the entire family," said all the poplars.

Chapter 10

By the following summer, it didn't make any sense that the old willow tree was still living. The bark had fallen off in big pieces, the holes down below had finally met in the middle so now a fox could slip in one side and go out the other. A mouse family had dug into the dry rotten wood, and up above, there were only three or four branches left, and they were so thin and lacking leaves that it was a very sorry sight.

But the garden up there at the top was just thriving as never before. The strawberry plant was erect with large flowers which became heavy, red strawberries. The black currant bush had also grown larger and was bearing its first fruits. The dandelion shone like gold, and there was also a little blue violet, a scarlet pimpernel that only opened its flower when the sun was shining brightest at midday, and a large rye plant that swayed in the wind.

"The longer you last, the better," said the wild rosebush. "Since you got off to a bad start by losing your crown, you must admit that fate was kind to you, and gave you some happy years anyway."

"I do agree with you," said the willow tree. "If only I can keep being happy. The wood in my trunk is 'getting thinner and thinner, and every year I have a few less branches."

"It won't end well," interjected the oak. "I warned you about my poor old hollowed-out relative."

"It's going to end like it always does," said the elder bush. "However, the end comes, it makes no difference to us. But I do think that the willow tree still has some good times ahead."

"It's no longer clear that it is a relative of ours," said the nearest poplar. "Its own branches are withering more and more, and it has only weird twigs and leaves left to flutter. That's just fine. Let's not say any more about it being in the family... let's be quiet!"

"Quiet...quiet...quiet," whispered down the long carriageway.

One evening, an earthworm crawled to the surface of the willow tree's garden. Up until now, it had always stayed underground for fear of the many birds that came to feed. It was as fat and thick and long as an earthworm anywhere in the world.

"Gracious me, hello dear earthworm," said the willow tree. "I certainly knew that you were here, but I've never before had the pleasure of seeing you. It pleases me that you thrived as my guest. How did you manage to get up here?"

"It was the blackbird," said the earthworm. "He dropped me from his beak. Actually, he only took about half of me; the rest of me dug back into the earth. So, I was really only half a creature when I landed up in your crown."

"You were welcome anyway," said the willow tree. "It makes no difference to me whether you're whole or half. I've lost my own crown, of course, and I'll never be anything but a poor cripple. But how have you managed to recover after your accident?"

"It's in my nature," said the earthworm, "and it doesn't bother me in the least if I get chopped in half; what's left of me grows right out again if I just have the chance to go around in peace. But do you know this little green shoot growing up right next to me? It has such a funny thick hat on it."

"I don't know that one," said the willow tree. "Through the years, I've lost track of things, have become less attentive, and I can't really keep up on everything growing inside me. Do you know what it is?"

"Well yes," said the earthworm. "I actually dragged it myself down into the ground two years ago. It was attached to a tender shoot and a leaf, and I ate them, but I couldn't get the better of the creature itself. That wasn't actually so strange since it was an acorn. Now it's germinating and it's a little oak sapling."

"An oak!" said the willow tree very respectfully.

"It blew over here during a hard storm in the fall a couple of years ago," said the earthworm. "I remember it so clearly because you creaked so much that I thought it was the end for all of us."

"What's that you're talking about," said the oak tree on the little hill in the field. "Is one of my offspring growing in you?"

"Yes," said the old willow tree. "It's really a little oak tree, and it's a great honor for me."

"It's a crazy world," said the oak tree. "It will die of course."

"We'll all die someday," said the elder bush.

Chapter 11

One day the master came strolling down the carriageway. He had his own two children, a little boy and a little girl, and the groundskeeper walking with him. They had only been at the estate a short time having traveled from Italy, and so were looking around with some curiosity because everything seemed new to them.

"What in the world is this old, ugly stump doing here?" said the master pointing with his walking cane to the old willow tree. "It's ruining the whole carriageway. Make sure that you take it down tomorrow, groundskeeper. I can't stand to look at it," he said, because it was just the way he was feeling that day.

"It's coming now," said the oak tree. "That was your death sentence, old willow tree. But, don't be sorry about it. Better to go that way than to remain standing only to hollow out more day after day."

"I'd rather stay alive," the willow tree said sorrowfully. "And what's going to happen to all my lodgers?"

"They have to be happy for the time they've had," said the wild rosebush.

"Now let's just wait and see what happens," said the elder bush. "I've expereinced worse things, and yet managed to slip away from them."

"Thank heaven, it's all over," said the nearest standing poplar.

"Thank heaven... thank heaven... thnk heaven," echoed down the long carriageway.

The groundskeeper came the next morning. He had only an axe with him, thinking it would only take a few strokes to fell that old, rotten stump left from the willow tree. Just as he was about to chip away at it, he saw the black currant bush growing up at the top. It had large, ripe currants. He stretched out his hand, picked one of them and ate it.

"That's really remarkable," he said. "It tastes just like the currants growing over at the master's garden. Who knows how it got up there?"

"Groundskeeper! Groundskeeper!" came a voice not too far away. It was the master's son running in the carriageway. He wanted to watch the old willow tree being felled.

The groundskeeper told him about the black currants, picked one, and gave it to him.

"Lift me up; I want to pluck one myself," said the boy.

The groundskeeper lifted him up and the boy wrapped both hands around the willow branches up above, but he grabbed so hard that some of the branches broke. Quickly, he reached out to the tree's thin trunk, but it was so fragile that he ended up holding a piece of the trunk in each hand.

Worried that he might have hurt himself, the groundskeeper lowered the boy to the ground, but his little face was full of joy and amazement.

"There's a whole garden up here; pick me up again!" he ordered.

So, the groundskeeper settled the boy on his shoulders and when he saw the garden properly, he squealed with delight.

"Next to the black currants, there are the most wonderful strawberries. Then there's a little berry tree, a sweet, little oak tree and some weeds. There are five yellow dandelions and a rye plant. Oh, groundskeeper, it's so nice up here. My sister really has to see this, and my father too."

"Hurry up and eat what you want," said the groundskeeper. "I've got to chop this ugly old thing down now, and that will be the end of all your oohing and aahing."

"Put me down," said the boy squirming. "You mustn't chop that tree down," he said when he was standing on the ground. "Did you hear me? Don't you dare!"

"I certainly will chop it down," said the amused groundskeeper who couldn't stop laughing. "You heard yourself that the master ordered it."

"I'm going to run up and get father," said the boy, "and you better not even touch the tree before I return. If you do, believe me, you'll pay for it when I become master here someday."

The boy ran down the carriageway. The groundskeeper sat down in the ditch and waited, which he decided was the smartest thing to do.

"The kid has the temperament of the master," he thought.

"What did I tell you," said the elder bush. "You should always listen to those who know what they are talking about."

"It's terribly exciting to be in the middle of this," said the willow tree. "If only I don't crumble into pieces from sheer anxiety. The boy already took a big chunk out of me, and heavens... there isn't much left of me."

"Now you need to hold out long enough until we see what's going to happen," said the wild rosebush. "I've never experienced anything quite so exciting."

"Neither have I," said the oak tree. "But you can't expect a good outcome when you're already hollowed out."

Arriving with his father, the little boy pointed at the decrepit willow and started talking, while the groundskeeper rolled a large boulder in place, so the master could stand on it and peek into the top of the willow tree.

"Amazing, I've never seen the likes of it," he said. "It's really true... there's a whole garden up here, and goodness gracious, even my own favorite strawberry variety."

He picked one and ate it. "Oh, yum," he said. "It has the perfect flavor; I almost think it tastes even more delicious than those at home."

"Then do you want to chop this tree down, father?" asked the boy.

"I should say not," said the master. "What a great shame that would be. It's the strangest tree I have on the whole estate. Groundskeeper, make sure it gets a hoop put around it at the top, and put a railing around the trunk near the bottom so the animals won't rub against it or burrow in it, causing more damage. We really have to protect this lovely old willow tree as long as possible. I'm so very fond of it," which he said because it was how he was feeling that day.

Up at the top, an iron hoop was put around the trunk of the tree, and a railing at the bottom. Every time the master came riding by with his guests he stopped the carriage in front of the willow tree.

"Yes, the carriageway is indeed very neat," he said, "but they're just ordinary poplars. But here you can see something that is most unusual. Sure, it looks like just an old trunk from a willow tree, but come on over here, and have a look."

The guests got out of the carriage, stepped up on the boulder in place, and one by one gazed inside to admire the garden at the top of the willow tree.

"If the iron hoop wasn't there, I'd crumble," said the willow tree. "Such a lot of glory and honor for a miserable deformed creature like me. Imagine, the master actually climbed up on me to taste my strawberries and all his distinguished guests now get to look at me."

"It's unbelievable," said the oak tree. "It's exactly like there's a benefit for being hollowed out now."

"It's like a fairy tale," said the wild rosebush. "I'm going to tell every bird that visits me so that it can sing out for the entire world to hear."

"You're not saying a thing that I haven't already mentioned," said the elder bush.

"Now, in all honesty, wasn't it I that made the fairy tale possible?" said the blackbird. "But, I'd rather it was more like the old times when you could sit up here in peace and quiet. Now you run the risk every moment that someone is going to stick his head up here and say: 'My goodness' and 'ooh" and 'aah!'"

"Never in all my life have I witnessed the likes of this," said the nearest poplar. "Did you notice that the master just dismissed his proud mighty poplars? We, who have stood guard here along the carriageway leading to his estate, summer and winter, year after year, always erect and towering and he called us just ordinary poplars. But that disgustingly plain, willow tree, that old rotten misshapen thing. I can't believe we're even in the same family with it. Yuk!"

"Yuk! Yuk! Yuk!" echoed down the long carriageway.

Chapter 12

One fateful day in the winter, a storm came along that caused all the trees to creak and groan. Screaming hard, the wind rushed down the carriageway and all the proud poplars swayed like rushes. The snow drifted so high that the heavens and the earth seemed like one.

"I can't take this anymore," said the old willow tree.

So, over it fell, right down to the roots. The iron hoop wrapped around its top flew off with a grating sound, rolling down the frozen path. The railing was all bent and twisted, and the garden at the top was scattered across the ground by the wind. The black currant bush, the strawberry plants, the mountain-ash tree, the little oak, the dandelions, the violets, they were all blown away, and no one knows to this day what happened to them. The puzzled earthworm was lying just underneath a piece of trunk, squirming.

"I'm not going to last in this condition." said the earthworm. "It would be better to have been cut in two pieces, even in three pieces; this is much worse. The ground is as hard as iron, and not a hole to crawl into. The cold bites into my thin skin."

"Goodbye to all of you. My time is up."

Well into the spring, the stump of the willow tree was cleared away, but the master ordered that no new tree be planted in its place. Every time he drove by, he told those riding with him the story of the strange old willow tree that housed an entire garden of its own in its hollowed-out top.

And the wild rosebush related the story to the birds, who then trilled it for all the world to hear. The oak never did manage to figure it out, but the elder bush said that it knew it was coming. The blackbird was caught in a trap and eaten.

But the poplars are still standing tall in the carriageway whispering to each other, ever proud, but still feeling quite offended.

The Obedient Wind

Chapter 1

Things never went very smoothly, but the wind was having a very bad week. On Monday morning, the skipper stood on the deck of his ship, spitting into the water and swearing until the poor man was blue in the face.

"I've been drifting here for a week, waiting for an easterly wind!" he cried, "and every day all I get are winds from the west. The fish are rotting in the hold, and I'm getting poorer by the day. For goodness sake...turn around, wind."

"No, I can't," replied the wind sadly.

"You mean rotten wind!" shouted the skipper.

On Tuesday morning, all the buds on the apple tree burst into bloom.

"This is the most important day of the year for me," said the apple tree. "Whatever happens today determines my fruit for the rest of the year. Nice little wind, I have so many new and delicate flowers, so please be quiet today. If you tear all my petals off, I won't produce my apples."

"If only I could," said the wind. Then it blew a fierce gale over the apple tree, and all the white petals scattered into the air.

"You mean rotten wind!" yelled the apple tree.

On Wednesday morning, the miller stood next to his windmill looking at the sky.

"How about a fine, blustery day, my good wind?" he asked. "Today we're going to grind some grain. I'm not an unreasonable type, like the skipper; I'm easy to get along with. I don't care whether you blow from the north or the south, the east or the west, just as long as you blow. I can simply rotate the arms of the windmill to whatever direction you're coming from. But if you don't blow at all, I'll get very upset."

"I'm coming! I'm coming!" announced he wind, and the windmill started to turn.

"Nice wind," said the miller, pleased.

Then suddenly the wind said: "Oh dear, I need to stop!" So, it stopped blowing, and the long arms of the windmill came to a halt.

"Mean rotten wind!" shouted the miller.

On Thursday morning, a boy who had been very ill was peeking outside through his bedroom window

"What kind of a wind are you today?" he asked.

"I'm a very strong east wind," replied the wind.

"Oh, nice Mister Wind you need to turn around, or be still awhile," urged the boy. "I've been really sick, and the doctor says that I can't go outside if the wind is blowing from the east. I haven't hiked in the woods at all this year, nor used even once the wonderful new bow and arrow I got for my birthday. I want to go outside so much. Please, Mister Wind, don't say I have to stay indoors. I need to go outside," he repeated.

"But I can't help you," howled the wind.

The boy cried and stamped his feet on the floor.

"I hate you, you mean rotten wind," he said.

On Friday morning, the minister's wife was hanging up her laundry to dry.

"It's blowing just right," she said, "and my laundry will be dry by the afternoon. What a really great day for washing clothes and now I can go and do my shopping."

But by the time she got home again, the wind had turned into a real storm. The poles were knocked down, the ropes snapped, and the clothes were flying all over the place. The frantic wife raced around, gathering all the clothes up again.

"Oh, my clothes!" she wailed, as she looked down at the mess in her laundry basket. "Just look how dirty everything is now. I'll have to put them all back in the tub again. You nasty wind! I hate you!"

"I can't help it!" bellowed the wind. "I just have to follow my orders."

On Saturday morning, the dandelion's new seeds were ready to fly off to find new places to sprout. The fluffy balls were so lovely, each like an umbrella, waiting for the wind to carry them out into the world. There were many of them, all of them really pretty, and the dandelion was very proud of them.

"It's nice when your offspring make you so happy," said the dandelion. "I developed flowers just for them and kept them well-nourished until they could go out on their own. Come now little wind and help me send them on their way. If they just fall on the ground, they'll be too crowded and compete too strongly with each other. Then, they will become very weak and die."

"I have given each of them a parachute that will carry them across the field. In that way, my family can spread and grow stronger, with more and more dandelions everywhere. Come now, little wind and take them away. All I want from you is just a gentle summer breeze."

"I can't do it," responded the wind.

And the wind didn't move at all; there was not even the slightest breeze, and it was so still and quiet.

"You mean, rotten wind!" shouted the dandelion. "Yesterday you created such a storm that the minister's wife's entire wash was ruined, but today you won't even carry my light offspring a few yards into the field. Shame, shame on you!"

"I can't," sighed the wind.

Chapter 2

On Sunday morning, the wind was still again, resting behind the wooded fence that bordered the forest. Nearby a mouse sat licking her paws after breakfast.

"Such a lot of sighing, wind," said the mouse.

"Why shouldn't I sigh?" replied the wind sadly. "There isn't a creature in the world as unhappy as I am. I always seem to get it wrong, and nobody likes me at all."

"Oh, that's saying a lot," argued the mouse. "That's not how I think about you. I'm tiny, keeping low to the ground, so mostly you just go right over my head, but the other day, I heard someone talking about you quite differently."

"Really?" asked the wind, suddenly feeling a little happier. "Was someone actually saying something nice about me?" Who was it? Oh, please hurry up, and tell me."

"It was the poet," answered the mouse. "He was sitting here with his sweetheart, reading her some poetry about you."

"Oh, the poet," said the wind wistfully. "What were some of the lines in the poems?"

"He talked about how gentle you are, when you flutter around his sweetheart's cheeks, and play with her curls," said the mouse.

"Are you sure?" questioned the wind. "Only the other day he shouted at me because I made her nose turn blue with cold and messed up her hair."

"Well, he also mentioned something about how glad and proud you were when you tore across the ocean with all your might," said the mouse. "He said he really loved it when you caused the waves to swell with their white, foamy crests."

"Huh? Yesterday, he was out sailing," replied the wind. "He got seasick, threw up, and then he cursed me. No, I'm sorry mouse, but he isn't any more understanding than the rest of them."

"Well, since everyone is cross with you, there has to be some reason," declared the mouse.

"Oh, but there is, there is..." agreed the wind, continuing to sigh and groan; it was very sad to hear.

"Well talk to them and explain yourself," encouraged the mouse. "It always makes you feel better to get things off your chest, and you know I won't take sides. You've never done anything good or bad to me."

"But they wouldn't listen, and I'm the unhappiest creature in the world," said the wind. "Everyone considers me to be this enormous force, and they are always begging me to do this or to do that. But I am never going to please them all at the same time, and really mouse, the thing is, I'm only a miserable servant who jumps at my boss's command. I really can't do a thing for myself!"

"Really?" questioned the mouse with a thoughtful expression. "That never occurred to me."

"Well that's the simple truth," replied the wind sadly, still feeling sorry for itself. "Every day, someone is moaning or yelling at me just because I do what my boss tells me to do."

"So, who is this boss then?" asked the mouse, sitting up and taking more interest.

"Oh, it's the sun," replied the wind. It's responsible for the good and all the bad things as well what happens with the weather, but I get the blame."

"Is that right?" queried the mouse. "Tell me more about it."

"Oh, it's quite simple really," said the wind. "The thing is you see, I'm usually quite still and wouldn't hurt a cat."

"That's decent of you I suppose," said the mouse, before she shuddered a little. "But I should tell you that if there is one creature that I'd like to see get what's coming to him, it's the cat."

"It's never a matter of being nice or not nice for me," said the wind. "As I said before, I can never make any choices or do anything for myself."

"But why?" asked the mouse.

"Well now, it's like this. If the sun begins to shine down real strongly in the east, then I have to take off right away. That makes me become a west wind, whether I like it or not. See, it has nothing to do with me."

"I'm sorry, but I still don't follow," said the mouse, wrinkling her brow.

"Okay," said the wind, "the air that was warmed by the sun rises up. I presume you know already that warm air always rises up because it is lighter than cold air? That leaves a space with no air in it... right?"

"Of course," replied the mouse a little huffily, even though she didn't really understand. "but I don't really care about that," she added.

"But I have to care," moaned the wind, "because nature doesn't like an empty space where previously there was only the warmed air, and so immediately I get the sun in my ear: "Psssst! Hurry up wind and bring some new fresh air with you to fill that space!" and off I have to go."

"Oh..." said the mouse quietly, starting to work out what the wind was saying.

"And even if I've just managed to be quiet and rest for a while, I have to hurry up to fill that space. Or, if I've been blowing from the east, then I have only a moment to turn around and become a west wind again! Oh, it really is exhausting sometimes, and I don't know if I'm coming or going."

"Aha!" said the mouse, looking pleased with herself now that she understood. "That's how it's all connected. You do have to do what the sun says!"

"Exactly!" exclaimed the wind, looking pleased that someone finally realized how awkward its duties were. "I never know where I'm going until the order comes. If there's no warming going on, I'm quiet and have to be satisfied with being scolded by those who want me to blow and can't understand why I won't listen. Then there's the opposite if I rush toward the west, hearing nothing but a lot of curses from those expecting me to be just a gentle breeze from the east!"

"Well, that's not much fun," acknowledged the mouse.

"It's certainly not, it's just awful!" cried the wind, looking unhappy again. "But what about this? Old Mister Sun, looking down up there, decides to begin shining suddenly in one place, and it beams down very strongly. Well that's okay, but I have to charge immediately across the countryside in order to arrive in time, and that's when I become a storm. I don't ever like to do that, but sometimes I even knock over the poor trees, or take the roofs off houses. Then, of course, I also have to rush across the oceans making huge waves and all the ships get terribly angry; some ships even get lost at sea. They all scream at me, hating what I've done and blaming me when accidents happen. But still, there isn't anything I can do about it!"

"I can see that you have a rough time of it," said the mouse. "It's really the sun that deserves all the blame... not you."

"That's right!" replied the wind, very grateful that someone now saw the truth, "but everyone worships the sun, thinking it can do no wrong!"

"Couldn't you find someone to explain your situation to more people?" inquired the mouse. "I can tell the other mice but speaking to humans is what you should do."

"But who would that be?" asked the wind shaking its head.

"You should chat with the poet," replied the mouse.

"Really? Are you sure that would help?" asked the wind. "Why would the poet care about how all this weather is connected? He just arranges words, so they rhyme for his verses. In his poems he might describe me lovingly as a gentle, mild presence, but in real life everyone bends the truth a little! Would he really tell people that I'm just the sun's miserable servant whipping around from one end of the earth to the other as he sees fit? What do you think would happen to his lines of poetry if he did that?"

"Well, that makes sense I guess," replied the mouse thoughtfully.

"Listen to what the humans say," said the wind. "They're coming back from church. I bet they'll be talking about me, and then you'll see that I'm not making all this up."

Chapter 3

The wind ducked behind the forest fence, and the mouse peeked from under the leaf-cover of a nearby plant as the churchgoers were walking by.

The minister's wife and the mother of the sick boy came along. Also walking by were the skipper, the miller, and lots of others.

"How's your little boy?" asked the minister's wife.

"Thanks for asking," replied the mother. "He's making progress, but very slowly. We don't dare let him go out as long as the wind blows so hard."

"Oh, don't talk to me about that wind," huffed the minister's wife. "Can you imagine... last Friday morning I put my laundry out to dry and the weather was lovely, with a nice gentle breeze. I only went to the shops for a little while, but when I got back, it was storming, and all my laundry got blown around everywhere and I had to do it all over again! Oh, that mean and rotten wind!"

"Please excuse me that I haven't ground your grain yet," said the miller to the farmer. "It's not my fault. It's the wind; you can't trust it from one hour to the next."

"You can never rely on the wind, it's just so unreliable and totally unhelpful," moaned the skipper. "If you need it to blow from the east, you can bet your bottom dollar that it will blow from the west. If you'd like it to blow hard, it will be real still, and if it's supposed to be real still, we'll get a raging storm."

They all continued walking down the road.

"Exactly," said the apple tree. "Last Tuesday, the wind scattered all of my lovely blossoms."

"The wind is the world's worst devil," said the dandelion. "On Saturday, it refused to carry my seeds away."

"Did you hear all that mouse?" asked the wind.

"Well yes, I did," said the mouse, "and truly, I am really sorry for you."

"Now you know what I am required to do," said the wind, "and you understand that it's not my fault when I make such a mess. I just have to patiently accept abuse for my boss's actions, so I'm sure that you can understand that I break down once in a while?"

"Oh yes, of course I can," consoled the mouse. "Others couldn't bear it at all."

"Well I do give in sometimes," said the wind. "Even though I have to obey, I cry as I tear across the ocean, shriek past the chimneys, and whistle in all the cracks and crevices. You heard what they say about me."

"Oh yes, it's terrible to be thought of like that," agreed the mouse.

"Oh, it is! It's very hurtful when they talk about how terribly the wind is howling and how frightfully the wind is whistling tonight!"

"You poor wind," said the mouse.

The wind didn't say anything more, but just sighed. The mouse didn't say anything either because it didn't know how to make the wind feel better.

Suddenly there was a great commotion in the air.

"Oh, my!" cried the wind. "Well, okay! To the south? I'm coming! I'm coming!"

The mouse scrambled forward to peek, but there was such a violent whirling that the she was knocked sideways, lost control, and almost couldn't find the way back to her hole. When the mouse was finally sitting safely in her den again, she was shaking with anger.

"That beastly, rotten wind!" said the mouse. "Here I sit, listening patiently to its stupid stories, and then it suddenly knocks me over hard. I've never experienced such ingratitude."

Too Many Plums

Chapter 1

Once upon a time there was a boy who had a stomach. Now there's nothing special about that because most boys have a stomach. When I think about it, I don't know of a boy or girl who doesn't have one. So perhaps every child should read this story.

But this special story is about a boy who didn't always get along with his stomach, even though the boy was mostly good, and the stomach was always good. We've all heard about this kind of relationship before, two good people who didn't like each other, but this was different. Here's one person whose mouth was quite at odds with his tummy... and it all started with a plum.

The boy really liked plums as did the stomach, but the stomach didn't want to have too many at one time. It wanted six, but the boy wanted seven, and they were both really stubborn and neither would give in.

When the boy sat down and ate plums, everything went just fine for the first six. It thrilled the boy, and the tummy didn't need to say a word. Then the boy picked up a seventh and his tummy gave a lurch. Now he knew how the tummy would react, and being a tease, the boy yelled:

"Go for it, tummy!" before he swallowed it in one mouthful, the pit too.

"Yikes!" yelled the stomach.

Immediately, the boy got a terrible stomachache, and that wasn't all; his mother made him take some yucky tasting medicine. Yes, that was to help him, but it was also part of his punishment because he hadn't asked if he could take the plums in first place. What started out as something exciting ended up not being much fun at all.

However, just as soon as he was feeling better, he knew he wanted more plums as soon as possible. He just loved them so much and was sure that there was no way that a healthy boy would allow his tummy to bully him.

Chapter 2

One evening he was sitting on the front step and thinking. He had done his homework and had been down to the plum tree where he counted that there were exactly fourteen plums left.

"I will fight you twice more, dumb tummy," he said. "And if I don't win this year, then just you wait until next summer."

"I'm not exactly running away from you, little guy," replied the stomach. "Wherever you are, I'm right there with you. Incidentally, I think we'll meet up again at Christmas time with all the yummy things like honey cakes. Have you forgotten how much fun we had last year?"

"I haven't forgotten a thing," said the boy, feeling bad just thinking about it. "You're a disgusting, nasty thing, and I'll fight you until I die."

"Oh, you shouldn't do that," replied the stomach calmly. "You know when enough is enough so, if you're a clever lad, you won't mess around with your tummy. I'd thought you were smarter than that before you overdid it with the plums the first time."

"You're always saying that, and it's just boring. But I'm tired now and I'm going to bed. You can rumble on for your own amusement because I know that you do it only to annoy me."

"Well, like you have your chores to do, I have my own duties," said the stomach. "Listen, can I make you an offer?"

"If it has anything to do with only six plums, you might as well forget it," said the boy. "I've counted them. There are fourteen left, and two into fourteen is seven. I'm not giving in. So, deal with that, tummy!" scoffed the boy, not believing what he was being told, but then he got a little curious. "So, how would that work then?"

"I propose that you pay very strict attention to my business for one day," said the stomach. "Or, let's say for twenty-four hours, from one morning to the next. Then maybe you won't be so tough on me."

The boy pondered this idea and then asked: "Can I determine myself whether to have a tummy ache?

"You're in charge," said the stomach. "You do all the things that I usually do, and let's see how that will turn out."

"You're on!" said the boy.

They agreed to begin the following morning, and the boy dreamed of eating a whole orchard of plums

*   *   *

He got up early, and the first thing he did was to sneak down into the garden and pick the fourteen plums that he hid in a secret place. Then he returned to the house and, as usual, he drank his warm milk and ate his three dry biscuits before he grabbed his books and rushed out the door for school. But, just as he came to the top step, his tummy rumbled terribly.

"Are you completely out of your mind rushing your breakfast like that?" howled the stomach.

"Good morning, tummy," said the boy. "I need to hurry, or I'll be late to school."

"But aren't you thinking about the milk and the three biscuits?" groaned the stomach.

"What about them?" said the boy. "They tasted all right."

"Yeah, thanks," said the stomach. "But today, along with tasting and chewing the food, you've also accepted my job of digesting it."

"Oh," said the boy, "a couple of dry biscuits can't hurt me. How long will it take?"

"It takes until lunchtime," said the stomach.

"Then it will just have to wait," said the boy.

"I think you're crazy," said the stomach. "Do you think I can wait?"

"You'll just have to," said the boy. "I need to be in school, and dad says if I don't pay attention to my studies, I'll never amount to anything. So, we will wait with the biscuits until one o'clock. End of story."

"Nonsense," said the stomach. "Your father says what he believes, but you didn't tell him about our agreement either, I suppose. a boy is a boy, and your word is your word."

"Can't it wait until my recess?" the boy asked pitifully, sure he would be late as he stumbled along with increasingly terrible cramps.

"Now let me tell you something," said the stomach. "It may well be that you won't amount to anything if you don't pay attention to your studies, but you'll die if you don't pay attention to the biscuits. You've already chewed them poorly enough, but let me warn you that this is something you should look out for."

"I have eaten biscuits every morning as long as I can remember," said the boy on the verge of tears. "And I've never had so much trouble with them."

"No," said the stomach, "and that's because I took care of the biscuits and all the rest. Today it's your turn for the honor and the pleasure. But now sit down on this bench and I'll explain the whole thing to you.

Chapter 3

The boy obeyed but was very unhappy.

"Now look," said the stomach, "digestion—that's what it's called—is usually my job, but today it's your responsibility.

You eat to grow up and to be strong so you too can someday have a boy of your own to harass when he steals plums from your garden."

"He'd better look out," said the boy. "He'll be in for it."

"But, just putting food into your mouth alone is not enough to grow up into a healthy man," said the stomach. "That's actually the least. If it was that easy, you wouldn't need a stomach at all."

"If only I didn't have one," moaned the boy, thinking of getting into trouble with his teacher and his parents

"Enough of your wisecracks," snapped the stomach, "and listen up.

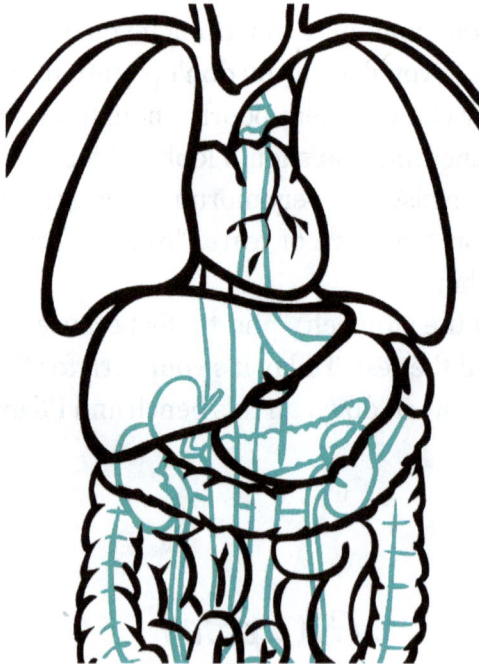

"Consider the biscuits. After you have chewed them and mixed them up with the saliva in your mouth, you swallow them, and only then do they come down for treatment. The more poorly you

have chewed them, the more trouble I have with them. I have to manufacture digestive juices which must be mixed carefully with the milk and the biscuits, and the bigger the pieces, the harder that is."

"When are you done with your lecture?" said the boy. "You're more boring than my teacher."

"I have hardly begun," replied the stomach. "When the biscuits pass through me, acted upon by my digestive juices, they proceed to the intestines where there are different juices I also have to make. They're the **intestinal** ones. They too mix with the digesting biscuits, and after that they encounter other things like **enzymes**..."

"Wait a second," the boy said. "Those are awfully difficult words; I don't understand what you're talking about."

"I'm sure it's hard for you, but you made a deal. Next comes the **bile** that also works on the biscuits..."

The stomach went on, and by now, the very confused boy worried about being late, and his tummy hurt so much he felt like crying.

"Don't you scream and holler," yelled the tummy. "It only delays the digestion."

And then the stomach gave a long lecture about the advantage of first lying on your back and then stretching and reaching and twisting the body in the weirdest ways so that the whole process could proceed satisfactorily. By the time the digestion of the biscuits was all in order, it was way past lunchtime, and it wore the boy out.

"Eat your lunch now," said the stomach, "and you'll probably recover."

The boy ate, and it also seemed to help, but then he realized how distracted he'd been and remembered school. Now he panicked.

"What am I going to do? What am I going to do?" he said tripping over his feet as tried to stand up. "I'll get marked down, and then what will I say at home?" He grabbed his books and ran off with the tummy screaming:

"Boy! Boy! Have you gone crazy?"

"What's the matter now?" moaned the boy.

"It's your lunch," said the stomach. "Are you going to run away from it like you ran away from the biscuits? You are dumb sometimes."

Chapter 4

So, the stomach started its lecture from the beginning again and the boy worked hard, watching out that everything went as it should, with his lunch being broken down by the juices and the enzymes—that were like mixing in some magic powders—so that the blood could extract all the good nutrients available. But he was soon heading for more trouble.

"How long is this going to take?" asked the boy.

"It will take until the afternoon," answered the stomach. "Do you still think I have little to do?"

The boy sat down in the bushes and cried, but that hurt. He dared not venture out before school was over, and since he didn't have a watch, he couldn't determine what time it was, and so he didn't arrive home until shortly before their dinner.

"Why didn't you come right home from school?" inquired his mother.

So, he had to make up a story.

"How was school today?" asked his father.

He was very sorry that he had to lie again for he was basically an honest boy who would never want to tell lies, unless he had to.

When they were all sitting at the table, he was so tired and miserable he couldn't eat a thing. Unfortunately, that day they were eating something he didn't like, and he got in more trouble because his parents thought he was being fussy. Now he felt desperate.

"Eat it," said the stomach, "or you'll regret it. You need it to fortify yourself."

"Not on your life," said the boy clamping his teeth shut, but no one heard the discussion going on between these two anyway. No one ever hears what a boy's tummy says.

By early evening he was feeling somewhat better but was still unhappy because he had lied, and his parents were angry with him because they thought he was being so fussy.

He went down to the garden and looked at the fourteen plums in their special hiding place. He counted them, but strangely enough, he showed not the slightest interest in eating one, let alone seven or more.

"Don't you want a little plum?" asked the tummy politely.

"Just you wait," said the boy angrily, making a fist with his hands in his pocket.

He was sure the porcupine would eat them during the night, if he left them alone, but he couldn't even think of taking a single bite. So, at supper time he ate his porridge because he was now feeling hungry, and then he went to the garden and ate the fourteen plums.

"Well," he said to the tummy. "I'm sure we will have a lot of trouble with you again, but so be it. I'm going to bed, and will probably fall asleep quickly, and then you can preach as much as you like."

"I'm afraid there won't be much sleeping," said the stomach. "We must work on the porridge, and I don't even want to think of how it will go with the plums. You know how badly it went for me when there were just seven of them and I was well prepared for their arrival. Goodness knows what will happen to you with the fourteen on top of a big bowl of porridge."

Never had the boy experienced such a night. His stomach rumbled and tumbled like a broken-down washing machine and he couldn't sleep a wink. He sighed and groaned; he tossed and turned, and he sat up and lay down. He walked about in his bare feet and got horribly cold, and when he got back into bed, the sweat poured from his brow. Every time he tried to close an eye, the tummy yelled at him: "What's this nonsense? You think you have any time to fall asleep?"

When his mother came to him the next morning, she became worried. "Oh, my, you look just terrible! What on earth is wrong with you? Is it your stomach?"

"I didn't mean it!" he said, crying miserably, and so she went to call the doctor.

"Well now," said the stomach, "the twenty-four hours are up. Shall we start again?"

"No!" groaned the boy, his arms wrapped around his body.

"Are you telling me it's better if I go back to my own business again?"

"Yes... please!" begged the boy.

"And have you now learned that I have enough to do so I can't possibly digest all the plums that a boy can think of eating?"

"Yes," replied the boy miserably.

"And so, you'll be happy with just six plums at a time in the future?"

"There are no plums left, and I never want to eat another plum in my life!" replied the boy.

"Oh, I'm sure you will when the plums come next summer," replied the stomach. "But if you hurt me with too many again, you will have nothing but trouble."

From that day on, the boy and his tummy were great friends, and perhaps you'll remember this story the next time you think about eating too many plums (or anything else) because you never have to worry about your stomach.

Thanks for reading this book!

Will you now please write a review.

Authors (and translators) love hearing
from their readers.

To help other readers and children find these
realistic descriptions of nature by Carl Ewald,
let the translator know what you thought
about the stories in this book.

Leave an honest review on Amazon or Goodreads or
your other preferred online store.

(If you are under 14, ask a grown-up to help you).

Thank you!

P.S. Please mention what your favorite story was.

www.amazon.com
www.classicnaturestoriesforkids.com

www.ingramcontent.com/pod-product-compliance
Lightning Source LLC
Chambersburg PA
CBHW070932030426
42336CB00014BA/2636